AN ENDLESS VIEW

THE ARTIST AND EXMOOR

SIR ALFRED MUNNINGS

The Barle at Withypool – Sunset

Oil on canvas

THE MUNNINGS TRUSTEES, DEDHAM

AN ENDLESS VIEW

THE ARTIST AND EXMOOR

JOHN YEATES

EXMOOR BOOKS

First published in 1995 by Exmoor Books

ISBN 0 86183 284 1 (flexi edition)
0 86183 282 5 (cased edition)

EXMOOR BOOKS
Dulverton, Somerset

Trade sales enquiries:
WESTCOUNTRY BOOKS
Halsgrove House
Lower Moor Way
Tiverton, Devon EX16 6SS

Tel: 01884 243242
Fax: 01884 243325

Exmoor Books is a partnership between
The Exmoor Press and The Exmoor National Park Authority

The views expressed in this book are the author's
and not necessarily those of the Authority.

Title page cameo:

FREDERICK JOHN WIDGERY

Dunkery Beacon

Illustration for John Presland's *Lynton and Lynmouth,* 1918

Designed for Exmoor Books by **T**opics – The Creative Partnership, Exeter
Reprographics by Scantec Repro, Falmouth
Printed and bound in Singapore by SNP Printing Pte Ltd

CONTENTS

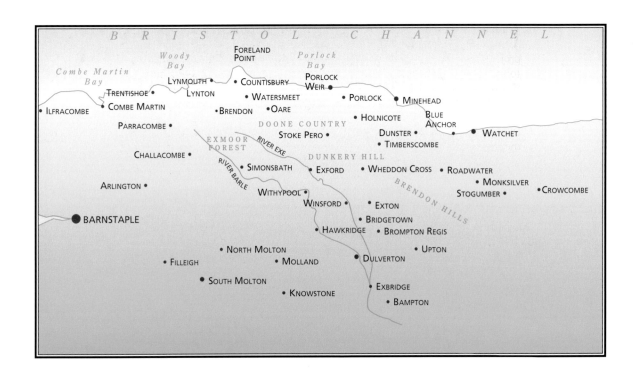

ACKNOWLEDGEMENTS

I am especially indebted to David Bromwich, Local History Librarian, Somerset, who gave much advice and assistance in the early stages of the project and to my friends and colleagues in the world of fine art, particularly John Biggs of J.Collins and Son, Bideford and Jane Baker, Exeter. Also Roy Heron, Sir Stephen Furness, Michael Webb, Charles O'Brien, Nick Potter, Rupert Mackeson, and John Mauger for his expert advice on the coaching era.

I would like to thank the many who have contributed illustrations to or allowed their copyright material to be used in this work; without their aid my task would have been impossible.

Thomas Agnew & Sons Limited
The Richard Green Gallery
Sotheby's London & Essex
Spink & Son Limited
Burlington Gallery
Ashmolean Museum
Birmingham Museums and Art Gallery
British Museum
Devon & Exeter Institution
Devon Record Office, Exeter
Museum of North Devon, Barnstaple
The Sir Alfred Munnings Trust
The National Library of Wales
The National Trust
The National Museums & Galleries on Merseyside
Local History Library, Taunton
Ordnance Survey Office
Royal Albert Memorial Museum, Exeter
Somerset County Council Library Service
Somerset Archaeological & Natural History Society
Tate Gallery
Victoria and Albert Museum
West Country Studies Library, Exeter

Also Mrs Jessie Lyne, Mrs Dora Biegel, Kenneth Edwards, Lawrence Fine Art of Crewkerne, Phillips of Bath and Henry Duke Fine Art of Dorchester. Lastly to my wife, Judy, for all her help and support during the whole of the enterprise.

INTRODUCTION

Loungers on the quay at Palma, Majorca in the late autumn of 1934 might have noticed a frail, silver-haired Englishman, with a clipped military moustache, being assisted up the gangway of a London-bound ship. The man was Cecil Aldin, the most talented and highly regarded sporting and canine artist of his generation, leaving his home of four years for a last visit to England. It was not to be. Aldin suffered a massive heart attack on board ship and subsequently died in The London Clinic on 6 January, 1935.

Why should a book about artists and Exmoor begin with this obscure tale of exile, return and death? The reason is simple. Aldin's lifelong affection for Exmoor helped to popularise both the moor and its culture through his pictures and writings. To Aldin, Exmoor was everything that a man and his family could want: the 'once upon a time country of our childhood imagination'. Roy Heron, Aldin's biographer, wrote in *Cecil Aldin – The Story of a Sporting Artist* that 'Aldin wished to return to England (from Spain) to see Cloutsham again, to follow the familiar Exmoor tracks and to visit all the places he was writing about in *Exmoor – The Riding Playground* of England during his final days in Majorca'. In the book, published posthumously, Aldin could not resist comparing the view from the terrace of his villa, high up on a hillside above the Mediterranean, with a similar view, 2000 miles away to the north, seen from the woods above the Anchor Hotel, Porlock.

Exmoor is, and always has been, many things to many people. Throughout its enigmatic history it has inspired the devotion of many and the denigration and despoliation of few. It is the purpose of this book to look at one aspect of the Exmoor phenomenon – that of its relationship with artists; what, or in many cases what they did not, paint and some of the reasons and forces which provided the impetus for their work.

The story of Exmoor is not unique; it is common to any previously inaccessible spot which has been 'discovered' and affected by the impact of tourism. The fate of parts of its northern coastline is that suffered by many coastal areas both in the British Isles and on mainland Europe, though, in contrast, the high moor has retained much of its traditional character. Some forty-one years ago in 1954, the wild heart of Exmoor as well as its picturesque villages and its unspoilt coastline became a National Park and this could well have an impact on how artists of the future perceive the landscape the Park was created to protect.

WILLIAM HENRY DAVIS

Changing the Horses,
Outside a Coach House of the Exeter and London Royal Mail 1821

The man leading the horses is Sir Henry Paton Bt

Oil on canvas
1015 x 2135mm

THE NATIONAL TRUST,
CALKE ABBEY, DERBY

CHAPTER ONE

THE ROAD TO THE MOOR

For many years the old Wills tobacco empire at Bristol was referred to as 'the sleeping giant of the West'. The same could be said of Exmoor. For time without memory it has existed, wild and unspoilt, keeping its secrets and discouraging casual visitors to its windswept uplands.

The northern coast is a different Exmoor from the high central moor. It is in partnership with the sea. The fast-flowing rivers which rise on the moor run through combes and cleaves to tiny beaches and habitable bays along the Bristol Channel shore. The coastal villages look northwards to the outside world and once reared a seafaring people. Until the last century there was a thriving coastal trade with Ireland, Northern France, Wales and Cornwall. Over the years commodities such as dried fish, oak bark (for tanning), butter, eggs, cattle and sheep were exported while imports included coal, salt, wine and goods to be sold at local fairs and markets. For centuries the Exmoor woollen industry provided a considerable two-way trade in raw wool and finished cloth.

Exmoor farms were worked by families without hired help and produced, in addition to wool, store cattle, young stock and ponies, serving the markets of Dunster, South Molton, Wiveliscombe, Bampton, Tiverton and Taunton. Bampton Fair, held on the last Thursday in October, was the principal horse and pony fair for the region.

For many centuries the centre of Exmoor was a Royal Forest, intended for hunting but exploited primarily for the grazing of sheep, cattle and horses. The land around the Forest was gradually taken into cultivation eventually becoming the property of the great Exmoor families: Acland, Bampfylde, Fortescue, Pollard, Heathcoat and Chichester. In the early nineteenth century the Royal Forest was sold, enclosed and turned over to agriculture giving us the moor much as it is today; an area of wild, windswept upland, bounded on the north by the natural coastal strip and the Bristol Channel, to the south and west by fertile farming land and to the east by the Stogumber valley and the Quantock Hills. Apart from a few small villages and isolated hamlets the moor is left to the farmers, the native red deer and ponies, together with large quantities of grazing sheep and cattle.

Until the nineteenth century, the high moor was only accessible on foot or horseback and, in the case of the casual visitor, a guide was essential. The first wheeled vehicles appeared on the moor in the 1830s, at the time as great an innovation as the farm machinery of more recent years. Before then sledges and pack ponies were the only forms of transport available. Greenwood's map of 1822 shows a road layout on Exmoor similar to that of today. In reality there were no roads, only muddy tracks and narrow unmade lanes, totally unsuitable for any wheeled vehicle.

The Exmoor pony was bred for hard work in harsh conditions, sure footed and good looking with a good shoulder and capable of trotting well. Celia Fiennes riding back from her tour of Cornwall in 1698 saw the harvest being brought in on the back of massively laden pack ponies. They were worked nine to a string and carried an average load of 240 pounds each, transporting everything from manure to the fields to produce for market during an eight or nine hour working day. Other ponies were broken and put under the saddle for rough riding on the moor.

The arrival of the first visitors to the North Devon and Somerset coasts in the second part of the eighteenth century was facilitated by an improvement in the road system both nationally and in the area surrounding Exmoor, during the earlier part of the century. Turnpike roads, properly surfaced, linked towns like Taunton, Exeter and Barnstaple with Minehead, Dulverton, South Molton and Ilfracombe. With the improvement in roads came innovation in coach-building and soon a coaching system, for carrying mail as well as passengers and small amounts of goods, spread over the country.

In the early years of the century it took five days to travel from London to Exeter. This was subsequently reduced to three days with nightly stop-overs at Andover and Ilminster. At the end of the century such was the improvement in roads and coaching technology that the whole journey was accomplished by the 'Quicksilver' in fourteen hours fifty minutes non-stop, other than for the changing of horses. William Henry Davis (c.1795–1885) captured the drama of 'changing horses' on a large canvas now at Calke Abbey, Derby.

A wide selection of road books was published to inform the coach traveller of the route, cumulative mileage, principal houses and monuments. The market leader in this field was Paterson of London. The eighteenth edition of his classic *Road Book* published in 1829 gives an impressive commentary of the 173 miles of road between Hyde Park Corner and Exeter. The painter J.M.W.Turner, in 1811, preferred to use the smaller and less informative Coltman's *British Itinerary and Principal Crossroads of Great Britain* when travelling from London to Exeter. While short on detail, Coltman's publication had, from Turner's point of view, one great practical advantage. It was pocket-sized and being interleaved with blank pages could be used as both notebook and sketchbook.

At the end of the 1700s a traveller to the South West in a hurry would take the 'Quicksilver' Royal Mail to Exeter and on to Devonport. Starting at the Swan with Two Necks, Lad Lane, in the City of London, it made its way via Piccadilly to Hyde Park Corner, leaving London on the Bath road, turning south at Hounslow to Bagshot, Hook, Basingstoke and then along the edge of Salisbury Plain to Andover, Salisbury, Blandford, Dorchester, Axminster and Honiton reaching Exeter (173 miles) each

CECIL ALDIN

The Quicksilver Coach
From, *The Romance of the Road,* 1928

day promptly at 9.30pm. The 'Defiance' and the 'Telegraph' took a shorter (168 miles) more hilly route from Andover through Amesbury, Wincanton, Ilchester and Honiton. The 'Telegraph' completed its journey in about eighteen hours, the more leisurely 'Defiance' taking an hour longer. Each coach had about two dozen changes of horse.

Alternatively, the traveller might take the London–Barnstaple coach along a route of approximately 192½ miles which followed the Exeter coach as far as Andover and then travelled northwards through Winterbourne Stoke, Kilmington, Bruton, Somerton, Langport, Taunton, Wellington, Tiverton and South Molton to Barnstaple and on to Hartland. Given Bath's popularity as a social, medical and cultural centre, it is probable that some early travellers to the North Devon and Somerset coast would, in fact, travel to and from Bath via Wells, the Polden Hills, Bridgwater, Taunton, Wellington, Cullompton and Exeter, a distance of 184 miles from London.

Once in Exeter it was possible to use many of the local flys (flyers) which would go to Ilfracombe or Barnstaple via Crediton and South Molton. A Unicorn (a vehicle drawn by three horses, placed in the form of a triangle) plied between Barnstaple and Ilfracombe while by the later nineteenth century a four-in-hand travelled regularly between Minehead and Lynton.

While travel by road was so slow and uncomfortable it was common even before the nineteenth century for some travellers to reach the Exmoor coast by sea though this was not always much of an improvement. In 1807 Richard Fenton, a barrister, arrived in Minehead complaining of a 'head that partakes of the fluctuation of that element I have just quitted'. He was glad to travel on the next day by post-chaise. In 1821 the steam packet was introduced, carrying both goods and passengers and operating at first from the Cumberland Basin in Bristol to Ilfracombe. It later started from Portishead to avoid tides, but lacking a commercial hinterland and relying on a highly seasonal passenger service, it did not survive the advent of the railways and was sold to the Great Western Railway in 1884 degenerating into an excursion service, which, in various forms, is still running.

The coming of the railways ousted road coaches generally, though they continued to run between Minehead and Lynton until the 1920s. Although people were now able to reach the Exmoor coast and the southern fringes of the moor more easily, travel onto the moor itself continued to be slow until motor buses were introduced in the second decade of the twentieth century. Until this time, anyone wishing to visit the heart of Exmoor, whether to paint or for any other reason, needed to be intrepid and adventuresome. It is little wonder that most artists confined their attentions to the Somerset and North Devon coast until well into Victorian times.

Chapter Two

THE
AUGUSTAN AGE
The Eighteenth Century

In 1719 Sir Jacob Bancks, M.P. for Minehead, presented a fine alabaster statue of Queen Anne to the town. For more than 150 years it stood in a corner of St Michael's Church but in 1893 was re-positioned in the centre of the town in Wellington Square, where it stands today, a well-known landmark. The statue, in English Baroque style, is attributed to Francis Bird (1667–1731), an important sculptor and pupil of Grinling Gibbons and Caius Gabriel Cibber.

The statue at Minehead is an indication that even while roads to the area were little more than cart-tracks and the heart of Exmoor still devoted to hunting and grazing as it had been for centuries, there were influences at work amongst the landowners and gentry which linked the region, albeit unknowingly, with the national trends and fashions in literature, art, and architecture in what quickly came to be known as the Augustan Age.

Early in the eighteenth century England was actively developing a national identity and its elite saw the country as the inheritor of the Roman Empire. The concerns of these Augustan idealists were unity, social harmony, balance, correctness and rationality. They regarded Britain and her embryonic empire as the successor of the Roman Empire in culture, politics, civil order and religion. Order was the keynote of the new trend and the form and order of classicism was reflected in the visual arts. Painters, sculptors and architects strove to obtain correctness by using the ancient precedents of grace, harmony and dignity.

A typical adherent of these ideas was Lord Burlington who enthusiastically took up the dictates and designs of the Italian architect Andrea Palladio (1518–80), initially at his Chiswick villa and later at his London town house (Burlington House) in Piccadilly, now the home of the Royal Academy of Arts. Enthusiasm for Augustan ideals ran high amongst the Whig supporters of the Hanoverian Monarchy and patronage for the arts and architecture was forthcoming from such patrons as Frederick, Prince of Wales, and the Duke of Chandos. A whole range of buildings, official, ecclesiastical and domestic, was produced, the most notable being in Bath and subsequently, London, Edinburgh and Dublin.

Wealthy Exmoor families followed this example with a spate of building. Hugh Fortescue (1st Baron Fortescue) was first in the field. He consulted Lord Burlington on matters of architectural design and then proceeded to enlarge his family home at Castle Hill near Filleigh remodelling it in the Palladian style (1730–1740). (In 1934 much of the interior was destroyed by fire and subsequently reconstructed.) The grounds were landscaped in the Augustan manner and featured numerous 'points-de-vue' including a triumphal arch, a castellated ruin and a sham village, some of which survive to this day.

The Aclands at Killerton, Broadclyst, almost forty years later (1778–79), considered building a palatial house in Palladian style designed by James Wyatt but in the end commissioned John Johnson of Leicester (later county surveyor of Essex) to design a more modest dwelling as a 'temporary home'. The simple, rectangular, two storey house with plastered walls, flat roof with parapet and pedimented 'frontispiece' still stands though much altered and added to.

The Luttrells continued to live in the Jacobean mansion at the centre of what remained of their fortified castle at Dunster. Henry Fownes Luttrell in the mid-1750s extended the refurbishment work begun by Colonel Francis Luttrell in the 1680s and landscaped the site, adding a ruined folly on Conygar Hill and decorative features in the grounds. The Bampfyldes at Poltimore added an eleven bay stuccoed front to their home in the form of a south entrance. Later in 1820, the Chichesters re-built Arlington Court in the short lived Greek Revival style using the Barnstaple-born architect, Thomas Lee.

Churches were built as auditoriums for public worship and the administration of the sacraments and existing ecclesiastical buildings were adapted for protestant prayer book worship. Molland and the old church at Parracombe are fine unspoilt examples.

Painting in England was the poor relation for much of the early part of the eighteenth century, little being produced that had high artistic value, save in the field of portraiture. Fashionable gentlemen preferred to turn to foreign artists for paintings for their mansions, often building up fine collections of old masters. The stiff, dignified portraits by Kneller and Highmore of self-confident men in full length wigs were replaced later in the century by the softer, more flattering paintings of Gainsborough and Reynolds. At the popular level Augustan ideals were held in some contempt. William Hogarth and his associates resented

W. WATTS (after Feary)

Castle Hill, the Seat of the Fortescue Family 1785

Copper engraving

DEVON AND EXETER
INSTITUTION, EXETER

the fact that native artists were ignored in favour of their foreign counterparts. Britain was an increasingly prosperous mercantile and industrial nation – why depend upon degenerate European cultures for role models – why not create a truly native artistic tradition? This attitude resulted in works like the illustrated moralistic cycles, *The Rake's Progress* and *Marriage à la Mode*. Each series was fed to an eager public by enterprising print sellers and exhibited good, solid, moral values and the virtues of hard work and political integrity: values which fitted well into the spirit of the age. Paradoxically it was an age much given to enjoyment and entertainment. The wealthy travelled to London and Bath for the seasonal round of balls and in the provinces most towns could boast an assembly room like that at South Molton, added to the Palladian-style Guildhall in 1772.

At the time Exmoor's reputation was not one which enjoyed any great regard. In 1724 Daniel Defoe, a Londoner who had fought in Monmouth's Army, travelled from Barnstaple to Taunton while engaged in his *Tour Through the Whole Island of Great Britain*. He commented that what little he saw of Exmoor he did not like, and quoted the Elizabethan Camden, who called Exmoor 'a filthy barren ground'. Defoe was full of admiration for the lower arable lands through which the River Exe flowed, considering them 'cultivated, populous and fruitful' in sharp contrast to his view of the moorland. 'It indeed gives a melancholy view being a vast tract of barren and desperate lands.'

Nonetheless there were indications that wild Exmoor with its bare hills, rapid rivers and spectacular coastline was soon to become more popular. By 1791 Collinson, a Somerset local historian, writing of Exmoor, considered it 'a mountainous tract with great propriety to be called the Alps of Somerset, the whole country being a picturesque assembly of lofty hills exceeding each other' with access to these parts of the moor principally through sheep walks. Collinson was especially impressed by Exmoor's dramatic coast while the small church at Culbone and the surrounding area were 'as truly romantic as any perhaps which the kingdom can exhibit'.

One of the first well-known artists to visit the Exmoor area was the portrait painter, Thomas Gainsborough (1727–88), who spent the autumn of 1770 in Exmouth and then returned to Devon in 1779 for a further six weeks in Teignmouth and Exeter. About 1782 he made another West Country trip with his nephew and devoted assistant, Gainsborough Dupont (1754–97). Few details of this visit survive, but it is clear from the known contents of a lost letter that Gainsborough visited Lynton and may well have used the occasion to produce a black and white chalk drawing of coastal figures and boats, now in the British Museum. This drawing is a typical non-commercial picture of the type which Gainsborough produced for his own amusement and relaxation. He was forced to earn a living by painting grand portraits in the Augustan manner, but at heart he was a Romantic, having a sense of oneness and intimacy with nature. If he had followed these instincts, he

would perhaps have been one of our greatest landscape artists rather than our greatest portrait painter. The North Devon drawing captures the spirit and atmosphere of the countryside, rather than being simply a mechanical copy of what he saw.

Gainsborough typified the new interest in the area among the affluent cultured classes long used to travelling through mainland Europe on the Grand Tour. Even before the outbreak of the Napoleonic Wars in 1793 confined their activities to the British Isles and encouraged them to turn their attention to British scenery and antiquities, some visitors of an antiquarian turn of mind or in search of remote and picturesque scenery were already coming to Exmoor and were recording their visits in words and pictures. Their interest in British antiquities was stimulated by the publication of such volumes as S. & N. Bucks' *Antiquities of the British Isles* (1711–26) and local county histories. Towns and villages on the coast, beginning to suffer a decline in their traditional trade through the failure of the woollen industry and the loss of the American colonies, started to turn their attention to the provision of accommodation for these early tourists.

In September 1789, the Reverend John Swete (1752–1821), left his home at Oxton House, near Exeter, to travel to North Devon. While impressed with what he saw along the North Devon and Somerset

THOMAS GAINSBOROUGH

Coastal Scene with Figures and Boats

Probably based on the North Devon Coast

Black and white chalk drawing

BRITISH MUSEUM

coast, he was determined to take a guide and cross the moor from Lynton to the Fortescue home at Castle Hill, on the back of a local pony. His whole journey is described more fully in the next chapter but one gets the impression that he hardly, if at all, enjoyed the journey. Perhaps his views might be tempered by those of Gainsborough who felt that Lynton was 'the most delightful place – ideal for a landscape painter'.

Whilst the moor remained a wild and romantic place, it did not attract the artists searching for saleable subjects for the cultured visitors to be found in increasing numbers around Minehead, Porlock, Lynton, Lynmouth and Ilfracombe. These artists were looking for a volume of sales as opposed to selling the occasional picture of house and estate to one of the long-established moorland families. All artists want to sell their work and it is in their interest to produce paintings, particularly watercolours, in the style and of the quality which the buying public demand.

Hidden away amongst both Augustan concepts and popular artistic tradition was the art of the topographical painter. Topographical drawing had been introduced into England by the Bohemian, Wenceslaus Hollar (1607–77), during the seventeenth century. Whilst working mainly in London, Hollar found time to produce several views of Plymouth. Hollar's friend, Francis Place (1647–1728), the first Englishman to use mezzotint engraving, was one of the earliest of a long line of English topographical draughtsmen.

There is, however, one peculiar twist to the sub-culture of topographical painting. The English gentry, having established themselves in country houses surrounded by gardens and parks, often employed itinerant, mainly continental, artists who worked 'on the knocker'; knocking on the owner's front door and appealing to both his territorial prerogative and vanity in hopes of obtaining a commission for a painting of the house and its surroundings for a modest fee. This market continued throughout the seventeenth and eighteenth centuries together with that for topographical views of London and antiquarian buildings. The old and new landed classes wanted their estates, as well as their hunters and race horses, to be painted and so, to a certain extent, topographical and sporting art went hand in hand. An extremely good example of this type of painting is the set of four oil paintings at Dunster Castle depicting the Luttrell estates to the north, south, east and west of the castle. They were allegedly used by the land agent to indicate to his employers what was happening in each of the fields owned by the Luttrells at any given time.

It was however, the general view that topographical drawing was the province of army officers. In pre-camera days, topographical drawing was not only a polite accomplishment for ladies, but it was also taught at all military academies as a matter of course; officers being expected to make detailed drawings of military establishments, displacements, battlefields and other areas of operation, to supplement their written

reports. In effect, topographical art was mainly bypassed by the classical content of high Augustan Art.

It is somewhat quixotic that whilst topographical painting and drawing were regarded as a lesser form of art, scenery was becoming a cult. It not only provided artists with a good living but landscape designers, such as 'Capability' Brown (1716–83) and William Kent (1685–1748), himself an artist, with a wide range of commissions and enormous influence on contemporary taste. The new order dictated that Italy and particularly Rome were the role models, and enthusiasm for the Grand Tour continued; this, when funds allowed, required the service of a good 'artist in residence' to accompany the grandee on his tour. Such posts were filled by artists like the Cozens, father and son, who recorded not only classical remains in Italy, but also the mountains, caverns, waterfalls and spectacular landscapes of central Europe. These purely topographical watercolours, together with the oil paintings of Italy by such artists as Claude (Lorrain) (1600–82) and Salvator Rosa (1615–73) provided a good indication of the changes in taste that were taking place by the end of the eighteenth century; the movement away from classicism to romanticism via antiquarianism. The whole of this deep and profound shift in cultural outlook was not to be funded by the inherited wealth of established landowners alone, but from the spoils of a colonial empire and from the profits of the newly industrialised towns such as Birmingham and Stoke-on-Trent.

The lot of the peripatetic topographical artist was not an easy one. The change in artistic taste from classical formalism to romantic, naturalistic and antiquarian subjects together with the restrictions brought about by the Napoleonic Wars meant that artists no longer accompanied patrons on Grand European Tours. Instead they had to travel around those

ANONYMOUS

The Luttrell Estates Around Dunster Castle c.1700

The West view from the Tor

NATIONAL TRUST, DUNSTER CASTLE

THOMAS ROWLANDSON

An Artist Travelling in Wales

Traditionally this is a self portrait, but it has been suggested that the artist was Rowlandson's companion on his 1797 Welsh tour as the figure is unlike any known portraits of the artist.

Aquatint by Merks after a watercolour drawing by Rowlandson Published by R. Ackermann, 1799

THE NATIONAL LIBRARY OF WALES, ABERYSTWYTH

areas in Britain which would provide commercial and saleable subject matter. The Lake District, North and Central Wales and the North Devon and Somerset coast provided popular material with commercial appeal but the weather and living conditions were not reliable and travelling was difficult. A good indication of the conditions endured is shown in Thomas Rowlandson's (1756–1827) caricature of *An Artist Travelling in Wales* in what can only be described as inclement conditions. The artist, mounted on a pony of poor quality, is encumbered by a mass of professional paraphernalia and is obviously hating every minute of his experience.

The Somerset journeyman artist, William Walter Wheatley, employed by the Bristol merchant George Braikenridge to record the churches and antiquities of Somerset, wrote some sixty years after Rowlandson, 'I am just returned from an unfortunate journey I have made in the neighbourhood of Porlock: having to travel to the various parishes on foot with my bag and sketching implements, going over those hills (as beautiful as they are), the toil in travelling, the difficulties in finding the road ... I was overcome with fatigue, taken ill and obliged to return home. I am now very unwell.'

Towards the end of the century there was a great demand for prints to illustrate the numerous antiquarian volumes coming onto the market and fortunately there was a ready supply of prints available. The brothers Samuel and Nathaniel Buck (1696–1779) published their massive five volume antiquarian blockbuster, *Antiquities of the British Isles* between 1711 and 1726. Sadly it contained no material relating to

Exmoor and its environs other than views of Tiverton and Dunster castles. At a local level John Collinson's three-volume *History and Antiquities of Somerset*, was published in 1791 followed by William Gilpin's *West Country Travels* in 1797/98, Rutter's *North West Somerset* in 1829 and Savage's *Hundred of Carhampton* in 1830. In the main, eighteenth century copper plate topographical engraving tended to be stiff and lack animation, having the formal appeal of the earlier Dutch topographical artists. This fault can be seen in most of the published work of Samuel Buck who was both a draughtsman and engraver. His output was prolific and was supplemented, between 1727 and 1753, by that of his brother Nathaniel who worked with him on both drawings and engravings, travelling during the summer months to produce the drawings which would be engraved during the winter.

Such was the enthusiasm for introducing prints into illustrated volumes in a gentleman's library, that it became known as 'Grangerising' after the rector of Shiplake, Oxfordshire, the Reverend James Granger (1723–76) who was a true Augustan figure and both a biographer and print collector, as well as the minister of a small parish. He inspired many amateur antiquarians to enhance their libraries with prints and the filling-up of a 'Granger' became a favourite hobby. It became the fashion among publishers of antiquarian volumes to leave blank pages for the addition of engraved illustrations to supplement their text. The material used by the enthusiasts was of low aesthetic quality, but the sheer volume available was mind boggling. Horatio Rodd, a London dealer, issued a catalogue of engravings of portraits in the early 1820s which listed about 7000 prints. In addition, he stocked topographical prints specifically for illustrating county histories.

The main technical advance during the eighteenth century in the production of prints, was the introduction of the aquatint, which enabled the publisher to offer what was in effect a hybrid of a print and watercolour, clients thus purchasing a high quality coloured reproduction. Ackermann's *Repository of London* and later *Oxford* were possibly the best known of this type of print.

Of the Augustan Age one might ask, quite legitimately, what in fact was its relationship with the artistic integrity and work of artists who painted around the periphery of the Exmoor uplands during the late eighteenth and early nineteenth century. The answer is simply that it provided an intellectual background and standard against which they could measure their own work and in the light of current fashions and changes in aesthetic taste, adapt and modify their own styles and outlook to produce the type of work which was commercially acceptable to their buying public.

One artist who always gave the public what it wanted was the caricaturist Thomas Rowlandson, a man who loved life and was able to dispose of large sums of money with considerable ease. The more he entertained the public the more he earned and spent. To him life was one long cycle of work and enjoyment. He visited the continent on

THOMAS ROWLANDSON

An Exmoor Picnic

Watercolour

BRITISH MUSEUM

THOMAS ROWLANDSON

*A View of the Mouth of the
Valley of Stones*

Watercolour

BRITISH MUSEUM

Opposite above

JOHN WHITE ABBOTT

Dunster

Watercolour

ROYAL ALBERT MEMORIAL
MUSEUM, EXETER

Opposite below

JOHN WHITE ABBOTT

Horner

Watercolour

ROYAL ALBERT MEMORIAL
MUSEUM, EXETER

several occasions before the Napoleonic Wars, revisiting France in 1814 and Italy in 1820 in search of material for the fashionable public who were his market. It is not surprising that he visited the North Devon coast in search of subject matter and seems to have found what he wanted.

Rowlandson was a popularist and a communicator. Francis Towne (1740–1816) and his pupil, John White Abbott (1763–1851), were Augustan purists. Both were born in Exeter and spent most of their lives there. Abbott inherited the estate at Fordlands, near Exeter and became a Deputy Lieutenant for the County of Devon in 1835. Each painted in an economic and individual style relying on pen outlines and flat colour washes. Whilst Towne travelled extensively in Switzerland, Italy and the English Lakes, Abbott only left the West Country once, to visit Scotland and the north of England.

JOHN WHITE ABBOTT

Dulverton, 29 May 1800

Watercolour

VICTORIA AND ALBERT
MUSEUM

In the spirit of the age the great moorland families produced amateur painters of some distinction. These included Coplestone Warre Bampfylde (1720–91) who worked both in oils and watercolours and was also an etcher of some distinction. Bampfylde was born (only son of John Bampfylde M.P.) and lived just outside Taunton as a landed gentleman, at Hestercombe House. He was an honorary exhibitor at both the Royal Society of Arts and the Royal Academy, where he showed highly competent local views and fanciful Mediterranean landscapes in the manner of Vernet and William Marlow. The National Trust owns several good examples of Bampfylde's work (Stourhead, Wiltshire). A large number of his drawings and watercolours were sold at the dispersal sale of Hestercombe House in October 1872, although some of his watercolours of the Hestercombe gardens remain in the house.

The Aclands, too, produced, over several generations, a series of excellent amateur painters including Sir Thomas Dyke Acland (1787–1871), Hugh Dyke Acland (1778–1836), Caroline Acland (fl.1820) and Sir Henry Wentworth Acland (1815–1900), son of Sir Thomas Dyke Acland and friend of John Ruskin. Sir Thomas's mother, Henrietta (d.1841), and his stepfather, Matthew Fortescue (1754–1842, brother of the first Lord Fortescue at Castle Hill), were taught to sketch by Francis Nicholson (1753–1844) and became enthusiastic painters. Nicholson often visited Holnicote, instructed Thomas and his brothers in drawing and produced several watercolours of the Dunster area.

JOHN WHITE ABBOTT

Lynmouth, 5 October 1811

Watercolour

VICTORIA AND ALBERT MUSEUM

FRANCIS TOWNE

Combe Martin

Pen, ink and grey wash
235 x 335mm

THOMAS AGNEW AND SONS, LONDON

FRANCIS TOWNE

*View of Porlock Bay,
4 October 1785*

Watercolour and sepia wash

VICTORIA AND ALBERT MUSEUM

NICHOLAS POCOCK

Dunster from Blue Anchor

Watercolour

BRITISH MUSEUM

WILLIAM PAYNE

*Lynmouth and the
River Lyn c.1820*

Watercolour

WEST COUNTRY STUDIES
LIBRARY, EXETER

GEORGE SAMUEL

*On the River Barle
Near Dulverton 1822*

Oil on canvas 890 x 1220mm

This picture was exhibited
at the Royal Academy in 1822

SOTHEBY'S, SUSSEX

Richard Phelps (c.1710–85) of Porlock was one of the few local artists to survive in the area during the eighteenth century. He mainly painted portraits and collaborated with Bampfylde, in addition to painting inn signs and repairing altar pieces. The Bristol Art Gallery has a charming conversation piece of the *Three Children of the Reverend Walter Brown, of Sutton Montis* and Dunster Castle holds several portraits. He was much esteemed by local families, though described by Maxwell-Lyte as 'rather indifferent'. Henry Fownes Luttrell of Dunster Castle not only employed him for portraits but also for the landscaping of the castle grounds which included the Palladian and Romantic mill bridges, waterfalls on the Avill and Conygar Tower, a sham castle.

Another West Country painter of interest is Nicholas Pocock (1740–1821). He was born in Bristol, went to sea and rose to become a ship's captain. Some time before 1780 he decided to become a professional painter, exhibiting at the Royal Academy in 1782. He established himself as a marine artist specialising in Napoleonic sea battles but also painted appealing watercolour landscapes in a naturalistic manner. He died in Minehead.

Possibly the best known of the West Country landscape painters is Samuel Prout O.W.S. (1783–1852) who was born in Plymouth and

PAUL SANDBY

A Road Near Ilfracombe

Watercolour

BRITISH MUSEUM

encouraged to paint by the then Headmaster of Plymouth Grammar School, the Rev. John Bidlake, who also encouraged the young Benjamin Robert Haydon (1786–1846). Prout developed a broad fluid style of painting, in the manner of Girtin and Varley, well suited to the lithographic reproductions which were introduced in the early years of the nineteenth century. He travelled extensively and was highly successful.

Another Plymouth-based artist, although not a native Devonian was William Payne (c.1760–1830) who was much admired by Sir Joshua Reynolds P.R.A. (1723–1792). Payne experimented with his technique, abandoning the use of outline with the pen and was considered by Redgrave to have given up topography for a more poetical treatment of landscape, though lacking the delicacy of the Cozens. Unfortunately for the reputation of the artist the 'Payne style' became corrupt through becoming too common. The judgement of the mid-nineteenth-century art historian and painter might sound harsh to our modern way of thinking, but by abandoning Augustan concepts in favour of a softer, more naturalistic approach, Payne verged on the almost sentimental in much of his work, offering rather sweet, sugary views in an idyllic setting and anticipating what was to happen later in the nineteenth century.

Paul Sandby R.A. (1725–1809) was another visitor to the Exmoor coast. A foundation member of the Royal Academy and drawing master at the R.M.A. Woolwich, he was an artist who had real feeling for the English countryside and considerable influence on topographical painting in the later part of the eighteenth century with a neat, fresh approach to his subject matter. Sandby is also important in that he was the second artist to use the newly invented aquatint method of engraving.

John 'Warwick' Smith (1749–81) was a protégé of Lord Warwick who paid for his stay in Italy (1776–81) in the company of both Francis Towne of Exeter and Thomas Jones (1742–1803). On returning to England Smith moved to Warwick from his native Cumberland and travelled extensively in England. Other visitors to Exmoor included the early lithographer George Samuel (fl.1785–1823) who exhibited watercolour and oil landscapes at the Royal Academy from 1786 until his death in 1823 when he was killed by a collapsing wall. A good example of his oil landscapes is *On the River Barle near Dulverton*. Another amateur at work in southern England at this time was J. Hadley (fl.1730–58).

By the end of the century, in spite of the difficulties of reaching Exmoor, many artists were visiting the area, however briefly, as the attractions of the coast and moor became better known to both painters and the first 'tourists' in search of antiquities and the wonders of nature.

CHAPTER THREE

THE ROMANTICS
TO THE EARLY VICTORIANS
Late Eighteenth to Early Nineteenth Century

At the close of the eighteenth century, a group of young, impecunious, Romantic poets were among the first aesthetically inclined visitors to Exmoor. Samuel Taylor Coleridge with William Wordsworth and Wordworth's sister Dorothy walked from Alfoxden, near Holford along the coast to Porlock and Lynton and were much impressed by what they saw. The Augustan Age was over and the cult of the Romantic and Picturesque was becoming well established. Mountain and moorland were beginning to have a greater appeal than the well-ordered countryside admired by the classical taste of the preceding era. From 1793 to 1815 the Napoleonic Wars prevented all foreign travel and access to the romantic scenery of the Rhine, Moselle and Switzerland so romantic scenery was looked for at home. Wordsworth's poetry drew his readers to the Lake District; the watercolours of Turner and Girtin promoted the romantic ambience of North and Central Wales while Sir Walter Scott's novels were soon to make Scotland one of the most romantic places on earth.

The purpose of the walk from Alfoxden to Lynton was to view the already popular Valley of Rocks and the trio started out one afternoon in mid-November, 1798. Dorothy Wordsworth recorded in her journal that the evening of the first day was dark and cloudy and that they had walked 8 miles to Watchet and found suitable accommodation. Throughout the walk Wordsworth and Coleridge were deep in conversation, planning the poem, *The Ancient Mariner*, which they began that first evening in Watchet. Coleridge had already visited the area and had written part of his great poem, *Kubla Khan*, at a farm near Culbone, though it is hard to imagine what the local people would have made of him, or for that matter Wordsworth, with their radical views and unconventional ways.

The enthusiasm of the three was infectious but transitory for they wrote little about Exmoor, other than in letters and diaries. Although William Hazlitt and Robert Southey were soon to visit Exmoor and Percy Bysshe Shelley spent a nine-week honeymoon in Lynmouth in 1812, the poets' initial enthusiasm brought no direct flood of tourists. However, their visit should not be dismissed lightly for these early exponents of English romanticism were in the van and their writings were to have far-reaching influence on attitudes towards the appreciation and conservation of landscape.

While the Rev. John Swete clung to the outlook and interests of the old Augustan days, his account of his journey over Exmoor in 1789 gives us a significant picture of the area that was rapidly becoming a centre for visitors in search of the Romantic. Swete travelled widely in Devon, using as his base Oxton House, at Kenton near Exeter, where he enjoyed the life of a typical 'Squarson'. A prebendary of Exeter Cathedral and the incumbent of numerous parishes, he was also a man of classical outlook and inclination, very much a child of the Augustan Age and true to his principles. His estate was remodelled in a style reflecting the prevailing ideas of natural beauty and order. A prolific diarist, he maintained a lively journal of his travels, illustrated with numerous watercolours in a style not unlike that of William Payne.

Swete toured North Devon in the company of two neighbours, commenting favourably on Barnstaple, as Defoe had before him. He considered it to have 'a neat and handsome appearance', but commented that 'the grade of the place is of late much reduced to the benefit of Bideford – especially in woollen manufacturing though other commerce continues, mainly consisting of coals from Wales, coasting voyages, but nothing of little import or advantage'. In fact Barnstaple continued to develop as a port during the nineteenth century later benefiting from its position as a gateway to both the coast and Exmoor for those arriving from the south. Somewhat tartly Swete commented that it was a centre of vigorous non-conformity; this, in fact, was so since Puritan times and the subsequent Act of Uniformity in 1662; little had changed since the seventeenth century.

Swete described Ilfracombe as a port of considerable coastal trade, possessing a herring fishing fleet and having a sheltered natural harbour, guarded on the seaward side by a large rock. It remained like this until the early 1800s when it began to develop into a popular holiday resort with rows of houses in the classical style, all stuccoed, neat and handsome with substantial pillars. Its first hotel was built early in the century and by 1825 the town could boast a ladies' bathing beach. Fanny Burney told her undergraduate son in 1817 that Ilfracombe had cheap lodgings but had become crowded. The Rev. B. Woolcombe, writing in 1816, described the donkey chairs used as a local taxi service for visitors and residents in Ilfracombe and the Unicorn (three-horse coach) used to convey visitors to and from Barnstaple. By 1850 the population had doubled compared with 1800, with the growth of

ANONYMOUS

The Valley of Rocks, Lynton c.1790

Copper engraving

Compare this typical stiff topographical engraving with the uninhibited version by Thomas Rowlandson

DEVON AND EXETER INSTITUTION, EXETER

seasonal prosperity and it was attracting the fashionable as well as the cultured. It was, and is, a beautiful place with easy access to Exmoor and fine views from the cliff tops.

Combe Martin and Parracombe both impressed Swete, though he was rather put out by the rapid and stony descent into Parracombe. He was particularly enamoured by the village of Lynton which stands on a hill above Lynmouth. Like Ilfracombe the villages grew rapidly between 1830 and 1850, accommodation being provided for the ever-increasing number of holiday makers who were discovering the pleasures of the sea, fashionable social life and the beauties of the surrounding steep-sided river valleys, hills and coast. Swete, sitting on a rock one evening, wrote, 'Why I ran over one of the most grand, wild and picturesque scenes conceivable. Towards the east it looked down a rough, deep precipice to the sea, and to the west it dwelt on the woodland recesses, the rocks and the waterfall, such delicious scenery at the twilight hour of calm in autumnal day has the most pleasing effects on my sensations.' The following morning Swete and his companions visited the Valley of Rocks, considered to be the major beauty spot of the area where 'the scenery was of a different kind from any I have ever met with, the hills first slope on towards the west, spotted with loosely detached rocks which in parts lay scattered about the bottom. Soon the tops of the succeeding hills became more and more wild and craggy – taking the shapes of disporting towers, gigantic obelisks and a thousand other fantastic forms – on the left barely at the entrance of the rail, rose in similar manner, craggy hills – the variety of their stupendous rugged frames together with those rocky fragments roll into the narrow plain struck me with amazement.' Given such a powerful impact on the viewer, it is not surprising that the whole area soon became highly popular with peripatetic topographical artists who found a ready market for their products, and this, in the main, would account for the large volume of watercolours produced in and around Lynmouth. The place was attractive and paintings were saleable. What more could an artist ask?

Having exhausted the delights of Lynton and Lynmouth, Swete and his companions took ponies and a guide to cross the moor to Castle Hill, the home of the Fortescues. The journey over the open moorlands was accepted as a necessary antecedent to the delights of Castle Hill. Whilst not being entertained by the family, Swete and his companions were greatly impressed by the house and its location. The party then journeyed on to South Molton which they found somewhat distasteful. It had, no doubt, already begun the decline which was to continue until 1850 when only one of the many woollen mills remained as a reminder of the area's once considerable industry.

Later, in 1796, Swete again visited Exmoor, and this time approached it via Tiverton and Bampton. On this occasion he visited Dulverton, Dunster, Minehead, Porlock, Lynton and Lynmouth, Martinhoe, Combe Martin, Watermouth and Ilfracombe, producing his customary watercolour record of what he saw.

At the time of Swete's visit, Porlock would have been considered of little or no importance, its only interest being its harbour at Porlock Weir. Minehead, like Ilfracombe, had always been popular with the nautical community as a safe haven. Defoe in 1724 remarked that 'it was the best port and safest harbour in all these counties.' Like Ilfracombe, though a little later, it was to develop into a popular holiday resort during the nineteenth century, reached by road from Taunton as well as by sea. The first day excursion by boat to Minehead from Bristol probably took place in 1824. Watchet's business had also declined save for a few vessels trading up and down the channel but it was to pick up again in the nineteenth century. Blue Anchor existed only as a beach on which limestone was discharged from small smacks specifically built for the trade. Dunster, whilst strictly speaking never a popular tourist resort with the eighteenth-century socialites and intelligentsia, nevertheless had an indigenous life and strong character thanks to the presence of the Luttrell family who originally acquired the lands in the fourteenth century. In addition to developing the castle as their home and headquarters, the family encouraged the town's trade and woollen industry, building the highly attractive Yarn Market in c.1600. The town continued to flourish until the eighteenth century as a market town and centre for the import and export of wool and woollen goods. However, by the end of the century the town was changing. In West Somerset the woollen industry did not adapt to mechanisation and competition from the Yorkshire mills. A dramatic decline in the production and processing of wool was inevitable. Collinson writing in 1791 states that the number of habitable dwellings in Dunster had declined by over fifty per cent and many woollen workers had moved out of the area, presumably to seek employment elsewhere. To offset the decline in the industry, the Minehead Turnpike Trust opened in 1765 a vastly improved road system linking the town with Bampton, Taunton and Bridgwater. However, the turnpike did not arrest the general decline of the woollen industry and by 1800 the annual mid-summer wool fair was reduced to something akin to today's fun fair, providing pleasure, not business. A steady flow of visitors stayed at the Luttrell Arms, visiting the parish church, the castle and its grounds.

At the beginning of the nineteenth century changes began to take place on Exmoor itself. With the growing demand for food for an increasing population and developments in agricultural practice, the Crown decided to sell the former Royal Forest at the heart of the moor so that it might be enclosed and farmed. It was bought by John Knight, one of a family of ironmasters from Stourport in Worcestershire. It is not clear how he became interested in Exmoor and its potential and it is interesting to speculate whether the family might initially have visited the area as part of the newly rich enjoying the facilities of Ilfracombe or Lynton and Lynmouth. Having acquired his 15,000 acres, John Knight pursued an entrepreneurial policy, typical of the new breed of industrial revolution potentates, well used to managing money, machinery, men

REV. JOHN SWETE

*On the Barle Below
Dulverton 1796*

Watercolour

DEVON RECORD OFFICE

REV. JOHN SWETE

Dulverton Bridge 1796

Watercolour

DEVON RECORD OFFICE

REV. JOHN SWETE

*Bridge and Cottage at
Lynmouth 1796*

Watercolour

DEVON RECORD OFFICE

REV. JOHN SWETE

Combe Martin 1796

Watercolour

DEVON RECORD OFFICE

REV. JOHN SWETE

Minehead 1796

Watercolour

DEVON RECORD OFFICE

REV. JOHN SWETE

*Dunster Castle from the Inn
Window 1796*

Watercolour

DEVON RECORD OFFICE

and materials, with an efficiency which has seldom been equalled. He proceeded to drain and plough a large acreage for arable crops, raised beef cattle, sheep and horses, planted hedges and trees and made new roads. Initially the roads were for the use of his agricultural empire and subsequently they were used to service the mineral working activities which were developed in the Simonsbath area and which required firm, well-made roads for transportation to the coast. These roads were to make access to the moor far easier for everyone. In 1842 John Knight abandoned the moor in favour of Italy, settling in Rome where he lived until his death in 1851. He handed the estate to his eldest son, Frederic Winn Knight, who continued to control and enlarge it until, on the death of his heir, he lost heart. In 1886 he sold the reversion of the property to Lord Fortescue who integrated it with his adjoining Castle Hill estate, following Frederic's death in 1897.

One of the most dramatic and long-term effects of the Knight family enterprise was the introduction of arable farming to the central uplands of the moor alongside the building of new farms, mineral extraction and eventually sheep-ranching. These innovations, together with the enclosure of other waste land on the fringes of the moor, had the effect of reducing the land available for the grazing of the indigenous red deer. It was not until thirty years later that the full effect of these actions was to be felt with the virtual eradication of wild red deer on Exmoor. The herds were denied their traditional grazing grounds, but where presented with fresh grazing areas in the form of newly worked or expanded arable land and given the prodigal eating habits of the stags, the inevitable was to happen. Farmers in self defence undertook the destruction of the stag population and it was a common sight, when a particularly large stag had been shot by a farmer or one of his employees, for the carcass to be paraded through the village and surrounding farms on the back of a farm wagon. It was this indiscriminate killing which, in 1855, motivated Dr Charles Palk-Collyns of Dulverton and his associates to take positive steps to ensure the future well being of the herds and the maintenance of the wild red deer as a feature of Exmoor for the pleasure and enjoyment of all, by the re-introduction of stag hunting.

The cult of the Romantic reached Exmoor in the form of a new building – what Castle Hill had been to the eighteenth century, Holnicote would be to the nineteenth century. Sir Thomas Dyke Acland built a 'cottage orné' complete with verandas and thatched roof to replace the house burnt down in 1779. It was a house of charm and romance, burnt down itself in 1851, but recorded for posterity by John Buckler F.S.A. (1770–1851).

The period 1785–1851 was one of intense activity in the arts. The major force was 'Romanticism' which was ultimately to lead the Victorians into the varying paths of Gothic revival, naturalism and historicism and was to fuel the pre-Raphaelite movement in its various forms. The mid-eighteenth century Augustan 'man of taste' with his passion for

antiquarianism was succeeded by a different creature – no less dedicated – but with a different set of values. As a mirror of the age a new bourgeoisie, a middle class totally unreliant on inherited wealth, land, the established professions or established merchanting, came into being. It was reliant on manufacturing. These were the people who came to the North Devon and Somerset coasts from their recently acquired classical town houses and highly profitable factories. In addition to the picturesque scenery, social amenities and fashionable fripperies, they found goods and services in profusion, from the houses built by speculative builders to the cheap prints and lithographs made of the area.

Romantic art stood in total antithesis to the classicism of the previous century. Formal public order and the creation of a national identity gave way to the shifting sands of human experience and personal response to it. The artist's role was to maintain his integrity while at the same time sharing his views and reactions to the situation or location. Painting ceased to be a mechanical craft and, like writing in the hands of Wordsworth and Coleridge, became a vehicle of personal vision.

Joseph Mallord William Turner R.A. (1775–1851) epitomises many things about the first half of the nineteenth century. From early photographic realism he became increasingly absorbed by the impact of colour, form and emotion as demonstrated in the painting of the Bristol express locomotive on Marlow Bridge (*Rain, Steam and Speed*, 1844). Turner, though highly commercial as an artist, spent his life probing

JOHN BUCKLER

*Holnicote: South East View
1839*

Watercolour

SOMERSET ARCHAEOLOGICAL
AND NATURAL HISTORY
SOCIETY

deeply into his personal vision and inner feelings. It is ironic that this intensely personal form of romanticism could thrive in the harsh realities of nineteenth-century capitalism.

Thomas Rowlandson, the great popularist, on the one hand and William Blake (1757–1827) the great visionary, on the other, demonstrate how much the art of the period was responding to changes in taste and new technology in the reproduction of images. This coupled with the rapid growth of literary output and the printing industry, was one of the keynotes of early nineteenth-century influence. One could almost draw a parallel with the growth and power of today's communications industry.

William Daniell (1769–1837) was the son and grandson of innkeepers in Chertsey, Surrey. In 1785 he went to India with his uncle Thomas Daniell R.A. (1749–1840) only to return on the outbreak of war with France. He subsequently visited Devon and Wales in 1807, producing his massive *Voyage Around Great Britain* between 1813 and 1825. The

FREDERICK CHRISTIAN LEWIS

River Exe: Hele Bridge

Published in *Scenery of the River Exe,* 1827

Drawn and engraved by Lewis

DEVON AND EXETER INSTITUTION, EXETER

Opposite above

FREDERICK CHRISTIAN LEWIS

River Exe: Winsford Bridge

Published in *Scenery of the River Exe,* 1827

Drawn and engraved by Lewis

DEVON AND EXETER INSTITUTION, EXETER

Opposite below

FREDERICK CHRISTIAN LEWIS

River Exe: Chilly Bridge

Published in *Scenery of the River Exe,* 1827

Drawn and engraved by Lewis

DEVON AND EXETER INSTITUTION, EXETER

work was remarkable, not only for the high aesthetic quality of the aquatint illustrations, but because Daniell also painted, engraved and published the whole work himself. Each plate was, in effect, an original work of art. Daniell relied on a technical innovation of fifty years earlier, the aquatint, as the medium with which to produce the images. The project was started in 1813, when Daniell began his voyage, clockwise, around the coast of England, Wales and Scotland, beginning at Lands End and ending there in 1823. As he went he sketched and painted continually to produce the initial artwork for the project. The work took eleven years (1814–25) to process and recycle, the views of North Devon appearing in 1814 and those of South Devon in 1825. The whole undertaking is of a uniformly high standard, both artistically and aesthetically and is a classic of its kind; topography at its best.

About this time steel plate engraving was introduced, enabling a hard surface to be worked, with the consequent benefit to the print seller that a much larger number of impressions could be taken from each plate before it required either touching up or re-engraving. A little later, in 1820, lithographic printing on fine limestone blocks was introduced from the continent. The two processes revolutionised the print market, making a wide variety of images readily available to the general public at modest cost. The age of popular art had arrived. At local level the effect was dramatic, and during the first two decades of the century, a vast amount of material was produced relating to the North Devon and Somerset coasts, no doubt eagerly snapped up by the early visitors either to decorate their new houses in the expanding industrial towns, or to fill folios in their embryonic libraries.

The leading Devon artist at the time was Thomas Hewitt Williams (fl.1800–30) who contributed to the amount of Exmoor material available. The main supplier of prints to the local market was James Banfield of Ilfracombe who seems to have had a near monopoly of local publications from the 1830s to the 1860s, issuing edition after edition of lithographs and line engravings not only of Ilfracombe, but of the dramatic scenery around Lynton and Lynmouth, and, by way of a pastime, publishing books on the area, mainly written by visitors.

In 1827 Frederick Christian Lewis (1779–1856), a Middlesex artist, who often visited Devon under the patronage of the Earl of Mount Edgcumbe (Turner's friend and patron) and Sir Thomas Dyke Acland, produced 34 etchings to illustrate a large folio volume *Scenery of the River Exe*, published by J. & A. Arch, London. This was the first book of views taken from the Exmoor uplands and is of seminal interest to devotees of Exmoor. Even when first published it must have had an impact on what was, in effect, a crowded market. It was followed three years later by a set of lithographs, *Views of the River Exe*, illustrated by L.E.Reed, but the Banfield machine carried on producing for the popular end of the market a large selection of local books and lithographs, steel engravings and vignettes (a particularly popular form of small engraving with uses varying from guidebook illustrations to the equivalent of today's notelets). George Rowe, one of the artists employed by Banfield, published work on his own account from Exeter and Cheltenham, but apparently with little success.

George Robert Lewis (1782–1871), Frederick Christian's younger brother, studied under Henry Fuseli R.A. (1741–1825) at the Royal Academy Schools and had a liking for 'history painting'. Soon he became a topographical artist and accompanied Dr Dibdin as draughtsman on his continental journey, both drawing and engraving the illustrations for Dibdin's tour through France and Germany. The British Museum holds a small and particularly attractive collection of his West Country work.

Rock & Co. of London published steel engravings of North Devon at a later date, the 1840s to the 1870s. Catering for the tourist market, they no doubt reworked earlier material published locally. The company carried about 7000 titles nationwide between 1848 and 1876 together with booklets, headed writing paper and vignettes. Besley of Exeter also catered for the same market with a steady but limited flow of work from artists working in the area from 1853–76. Trix's Repository at Lynmouth was also active in the field but on a more restricted basis.

However, always in the background was the greatest artist of the day, J.M.W.Turner R.A., who was destined to become a one-man print industry and eclipse all his contemporaries in this field as he did in everything else he produced, from vaporous watercolour sketches to enormous romantic oil paintings.

J.M.W. TURNER

Self-Portrait c.1800

Oil on canvas

TATE GALLERY

GEORGE ROBERT LEWIS

Valley of Rocks
Watercolour

A picture to delight the Romantic visitor, down to the resting stone-breaker

BRITISH MUSEUM

GEORGE ROBERT LEWIS

Ilfracombe

Watercolour

BRITISH MUSEUM

Turner's parents came from South Molton, removing to London before his birth – part of the great drift to the cities fuelled by the industrial revolution. Turner never made much of his Devon antecedents, though he is on record as having once claimed to be a Devonian, but in typical Turner fashion, from the neighbouring town of Barnstaple, not South Molton, assuming that his acquaintances would not have heard of the town. Turner was born in London and had all the qualities of a Cockney: curiosity, forthrightness, quick thinking and an entrepreneurial outlook on life. To these were added formidable powers of observation, assimilation and expression which placed him head and shoulders above his contemporaries.

Always working as a topographical artist, his first major commission for prints came when he was twenty-three from the Oxford University Press for ten drawings to illustrate the 1798 *Oxford University Almanac*. Around the same time Turner produced artwork for prints covering the remote district of Whalley and Clitheroe in Lancashire. A gap of twenty years followed during which the steel plate engraving techniques were introduced and in 1822 Turner's publisher, William Bernard Cooke, exhibited, at his Soho Square Gallery, groups of drawings which Turner had produced for his publications between 1814 and 1826, including *The Rivers of England* and *Picturesque Views of the Southern Coast of England*.

From a commercial point of view many of Cooke's publications were unsuccessful and, typically, Turner transferred his allegiance to new publishers, Moon, Boys and Graves, and Charles Heath. Heath launched an ambitious project in the form of a 96-plate *Picturesque Views of England and Wales* – engraved on copper, not steel, plates. By 1838 it was clear that the project had yet again failed and Heath went bankrupt, though not before successfully showing Turner's drawings and watercolours for the publication. Despite these failures Turner was not daunted and continued to produce a large number of paintings for publication as prints, including *The Rivers of France* (foreign views having become extremely popular following victory over the French in 1815). Moon, Boys and Graves published Turner's Italian Views and in the early 1830s held several watercolour exhibitions of the original works.

While Turner allowed his watercolour originals for the engravings to be sold off individually by his publishers, he insisted on the highest quality of engraving and reproduction for each of the engraved images and went to extraordinary lengths to control them, even training a team of engravers to transfer images from his original watercolours to their printed form. Turner himself never worked on the plates, but always corrected and adjusted them to obtain the exact effect which he required. There are in existence large quantities of corrected artist's proofs by Turner, particularly in the Turner Collection at the Tate

WILLIAM DANIELL

Ilfracombe and Lantern Hill 1814

Aquatint: drawn, engraved and published by the artist

HEALE GALLERY, SOMERSET

Gallery. Incidentally, this is the true definition of the term 'artist's proof', a proof which the artist has personally checked and corrected, not the erroneous modern use of the term as a signed and numbered photographic print. While Turner was happy to have his originals sold piecemeal, it is obvious that he wanted each collection of views to be seen as a series and not individually. Each subject was carefully selected and treated with masterly precision to express the exact impact which he considered the subject merited.

It is difficult to know when Turner, or his publisher, conceived the idea of *The Picturesque Views of the Southern Coast of England*. The project must have been exercising Turner during his West Country visit of 1811 as the artist used the blank interleaved pages of his pocket-sized *Coltman's British Itinerary* as a notebook for the draft of an epic poem, juxtaposing scenic descriptions with both historical reflections and patriotic moralising. It was his most ambitious poem at that time. It would appear that Turner wanted his publisher, William Bernard Cooke, to include it in the publication as part of the text. In this he was disappointed. The text related strictly to the published images without additional comments.

Work on the project commenced in 1814, the same year that Turner's fellow Royal Academician, William Daniell, began his massive eight-volume *A Voyage around Britain*. Cooke restricted Turner's work to two volumes covering the whole of the south coast in a clockwise direction: from Whitstable, Kent, in the east to Watchet, Somerset, in the west. The work was finished in 1826. The views of the North Devon and Somerset coast number six. Ilfracombe, Combe Martin, Lynmouth, Porlock, Minehead and Watchet. The images of Lynmouth and Porlock were vignettes produced by Turner's collaborator, William Collins R.A. (1788–1847).

This was Turner's most important collection of topographical prints and one which called on all his impressive powers, then at the height of their maturity. His prints were supplemented when the need arose by vignettes, after the work of other artists, to ensure a complete view of southern England as a geographical entity. His prints presented a spectrum of land, sea and sky featuring a vast army of men, women and children for whom a harsh life under open skies on stormy seas, muddy roads and steep hills was a reality rather than a figment of a romantic imagination. They were an island race who had their business on great waters, who manned the ships of the British Navy, accepted life without complaint, when all too often they found themselves unwanted and neglected – only to be asked for more when the national effort against Napolean required it of them, or once the fighting had ceased, to fall victim to unemployment, economic stagnation and inflation. Each of the forty views was sold at a guinea and a half (£1.57) for images on India paper (a fine paper laid down on a strong supporting sheet) or 14s. (70p) for an ordinary print, each being a full plate size.

Turner used two bases for the major part of the project: the chaotic

J.M.W. TURNER

Ilfracombe: Hillsborough Cliffs 1818

Steel engraving

TURNER COLLECTION, TATE GALLERY

J.M.W. TURNER

Combe Martin c.1824

Watercolour 150 x 230mm

ASHMOLEAN MUSEUM, OXFORD

J.M.W. TURNER

Lynmouth

From a Devonshire sketch-book 1811

TURNER COLLECTION, TATE GALLERY

WILLIAM COLLINS

Lynmouth

Steel engraving

TURNER COLLECTION, TATE GALLERY

Opposite above

WILLIAM COLLINS

Porlock

Steel engraving

TURNER COLLECTION,
TATE GALLERY

Opposite below

J.M.W. TURNER

Minehead

From a Devonshire
sketch-book 1811

TURNER COLLECTION,
TATE GALLERY

household of his patron, the Earl of Egremont at Petworth, Sussex (who also owned Orchard Wyndham at Williton) for the eastern section, and the home of the Earl of Mount Edgcumbe at Plymouth, for the western section. In addition, he made extra trips to the West Country on at least three occasions, presumably to complete work on the North Devon and Somerset coastlines. It is probable that his highly attractive and innately romantic painting of Dunster Castle was produced during one of these visits.

Travelling to Ilfracombe from Exeter in 1811, Turner would have passed through South Molton and it would be interesting to know what his feelings were on the occasion. Certainly the fleeting visit went unrecorded.

On reaching Ilfracombe, Turner produced one of his most arresting images. Both Turner and his contemporary William Daniell produced paintings and subsequently engravings of the same landmark, Lantern Hill, the former island guarding the entrance to Ilfracombe Harbour and topped by a small lighthouse. Daniell remained true to the outlook and order of the Augustan Age, producing a calm, detached, reflective watercolour of the view, strictly an accurate objective observation, with no intrusion of his feelings whatsoever. Turner, who first established his reputation with a large canvas of *Dutch Boats in a Gale*, took the opportunity to create a minor masterpiece, giving full vent to the impact of the romantic movement and creating a picture with an almost Wagnerian visual impact. The view of the island is taken from the sea and, as one would expect from an artist who had had himself lashed to the foot of a mast on the Dover–Ostend packet during a storm to enable him to sketch more fully and accurately, nothing is held back, giving the observer a view of a storm seldom, if ever, surpassed in an engraving. A boat is being smashed onto the rocks at the foot of Hillsborough Cliffs and Lantern Hill is relegated to a backcloth, whilst at the top of the sheer cliff drenched onlookers watch helplessly. It was the complete antithesis of the control of nature advocated by the Augustans and a product of the eye and mind of an artist who could feel deeply and knew exactly how to convey the experience he had undergone to his public. We only know the picture from the engraving, the original watercolour being in a private Swiss collection and unavailable to the public and art historians, but this image alone justifies the care and attention which Turner lavished on his prints, from the expert team of engravers to the hours he spent correcting and refining their work. This scene was obviously a favourite subject for Turner, as he painted it in several forms, one of the best known, painted years earlier, being *Calais Pier* where the dynamism of the waves contrasts sharply with the panic-stricken fishermen struggling to prevent their boat being smashed.

In contrast to the fury and energy of the Ilfracombe image, that of *Combe Martin* provided a pastoral scene with human dimensions. We are invited to look along Combe Martin bay towards Burrow Nose. In

J.M.W. TURNER

Minehead 1811

Watercolour 150 x 230mm

NATIONAL MUSEUMS AND GALLERIES ON MERSEYSIDE

J.M.W. TURNER

Dunster Castle

From a Devonshire
sketch-book 1811

TURNER COLLECTION, TATE
GALLERY

J.M.W. TURNER

Watchet

The eightieth and final scene of Turner's tour of the south coast

Steel engraving

TURNER COLLECTION, TATE GALLERY

the foreground women are laying out washing to dry on a lime kiln in the early morning sunshine, while nearby a man pitchforks seaweed into panniers on a pony's back. In the engraving a small fishing smack has been added.

Lynmouth is a vignette of a painting by William Collins showing two fishermen on the beach near their boat, cooking a meal over an open fire. One wonders if Turner is poking fun at the earliest visitors to the Valley of Rocks and the Lyn Valley, who could have considered such activity crude and contemptible in the extreme. Daniell remains his impassive objective self, giving us a charming view of Lynmouth as a small village built on rocks beneath towering cliffs.

Porlock is again a vignette by Collins showing a view across the groynes with a beached fishing boat and fishermen mending nets. Again Turner is anxious to show the dignity of labour to his sophisticated audience and draw their attention to something they themselves might not have observed either on holiday or in the industrial towns from which they came. The picture was painted under Turner's direction.

With *Minehead* and *Watchet* we move to a more measured tempo. The former shows a sweeping view over Blue Anchor Bay to Dunster Castle with North Hill beyond and the Blue Anchor Inn in the foreground. The view of Watchet is enhanced by a woman working in the foreground as a sailor lies stupefied in the afternoon heat, no doubt sleeping off a serious drinking session at one of the local inns, before facing the

JOHN BUCKLER

Dunster: North Front of Castle

Watercolour

SOMERSET ARCHAEOLOGICAL AND NATURAL HISTORY SOCIETY

dangers of a further sea voyage. Here Turner ended his tour of the south coast, whereas Daniell had left the coast at Lynmouth to sail north across the Bristol Channel to South Wales.

It is surprising, given Turner's capacity for endurance and enterprise, demonstrated by his regular travels across mainland Europe, that he did not attempt to make the journey on the back of an Exmoor pony to the heart of the moor and treat us to his impressions of the wilderness which surely would have excited him as much as anything that he was to see in France, Germany, Switzerland or Italy. Perhaps it was the thought of taking the mandatory guide which put him off or else the need to return to London on pressing business. It is our loss that he did not venture from the coast.

A generation after Turner, John Chessell Buckler (1793–1894) practised both as an architect and a watercolour painter of buildings, particularly those with antiquarian interest, creating a detailed pencil image on location and working up the finished watercolour in his studio. It was his ability to produce superb images of churches and antiquarian buildings in the Augustan manner which recommended him to John Hugh Smyth-Pigott (1792–1853) of Weston-super-Mare, an interesting man who was the illegitimate son of Sir Hugh Smyth (1772–1824). On the occasion of his marriage to Ann Pigott and in order to secure the future of the two family estates, he assumed the name and arms of the Pigott family. In addition to being the father of ten children, a member of the Society of Antiquaries and a holder of county offices, he also promoted Weston-super-Mare as a holiday resort and took a lively interest in archaeological discoveries on his estate. He was a man of culture, a dedicated antiquary, artistically gifted and had the financial means to indulge his interests. For example, rather than 'Grangerise' his copy of Collinson's *History of Somerset* in 1827 he commissioned John Chessel Buckler and his father John Buckler to produce a set of watercolour drawings of Somerset churches, houses, monuments and seats. The end result of this project is the delightful collection of monotone watercolours owned by the Somerset Archaeological and Natural History Society, which is not only a wonderful and extensive record of the county's churches but lifts the corner of the veil to show us what the Church of England looked like in the days of Jane Austen and her contemporaries: simple elegant churches, totally uncluttered by the objets d'art introduced by Victorians. It shows something of the innate simplicity of the national church and protestant worship before both succumbed to the onslaught of Victorian romanticism in the form of a Gothic revival.

All the watercolours in the Smyth-Pigott collection are impeccably produced, both the artists, Buckler father and son, working together in identical manner so that only the signature distinguishes them. During his lifetime, Buckler senior is reputed to have made thirteen thousand drawings.

In 1825, a year before Turner completed his picturesque views of the southern coast of England and the year in which Daniell completed his

SAMUEL GRIFFITHS TOVEY

Interior of Culbone Church c.1840

Watercolour

An evocative picture of a church designed for worship according to the Book of Common Prayer reflecting Augustan principles of order and dignity

SOMERSET ARCHAEOLOGICAL AND NATURAL HISTORY SOCIETY

voyage around Great Britain, an event took place on the moor uplands which was to have a profound effect on the future well-being of the moor. Stag hunting ceased on Exmoor, though the country continued to be hunted by visiting packs on an ad hoc basis from time to time. One such visit must have attracted Herbert Byng Hall to the Exmoor uplands in 1849. Travelling independently, he arrived late one afternoon at the end of October, having left London the previous night by rail for Bridgwater where he then posted a fast horse to Porlock. Such was the impression that Exmoor and its sport made that he subsequently wrote of his adventures in a modest volume *Exmoor: or In the Footsteps of St Hubert.* In addition to the text, the volume is notable for its semi-humorous but sadly anonymous illustrations and gives some idea of what stag hunting and its related activities were like in the mid-century years.

Whilst Buckler and his father were working on the material for Smyth-Pigott's edition of Collinson's *History of Somerset*, other people were taking an interest in the moor, and in 1830 James Savage published his *History of the Hundred of Carhampton*. The single volume remarkably lacked illustrations, save for a steel plate engraving of *Dunster Yarn Market* after John Buckler. All that can be said of the single illustration is that it is far superior to T. Bonnor's line engraving of Dunster Castle in Collinson's *History of Somerset*.

In the 1840s George Weare Braikenridge (1775–1856) a retired Bristol dry salter and West Indian merchant, followed in the footsteps of his fellow member of the Society of Antiquaries, Smyth-Pigott and commissioned the West Country artist William Walter Wheatley (1811–85) to illustrate his copy of Collinson's *History of Somerset*. Wheatley was a competent journeyman watercolourist, painting what he saw in the best way that he could. Following the Bucklers' footsteps he produced a parallel set of watercolours for his patron, supplemented by paintings of churches which the Bucklers did not visit (e.g. Exford, Oare and Stoke Pero). Wheatley enjoyed a good relationship with his employer who required accuracy rather than aesthetic quality and was thus an undemanding patron. Wheatley, though of limited ability, was in complete sympathy with Braikenridge. This, allied to his intimate knowledge of Somerset, kept him in business for several years. He

WILLIAM WALTER WHEATLEY

Oare: Cottage Interior

Watercolour

SOMERSET ARCHAEOLOGICAL AND NATURAL HISTORY SOCIETY

JOHN BUCKLER

Dunster Castle

Frontispiece,
James Savage's *History of the Hundred of Carhampton* 1830

Steel engraving 65 x 95mm

LOCAL HISTORY LIBRARY, TAUNTON

travelled the country on behalf of his patron, painting, making brass rubbings and copying monument inscriptions while talking to church wardens and making notes on local customs. A prolific drawing master and conscientious draughtsman, he died in reduced circumstances. Braikenridge also used the Bristol artist of architectural subjects and Venetian scenes, Samuel Griffiths Tovey (fl. 1847–65) who, among other subjects, produced a charming *Interior of Culbone Church.*

Like the Smyth-Pigott collection, the Braikenridge collection is the property of the Somerset Archaeological and Natural History Society, though the Society of Antiquaries owns a parallel Wheatley illustrated *History of Somerset* in the form of the Adlam Collection. Wheatley also worked for the Rev. J.S.H. Horner of Mells. Included in the Braikenridge Collection is a rather poor but interesting interior of a cottage in the Doone Valley, the only known picture of a mid-nineteenth century Exmoor domestic scene. Intriguingly for a Bristolian, Braikenridge was of Scottish extraction. Like Smyth-Pigott, he had ten children, six of whom reached adulthood and none of whom produced children to inherit his substantial antiquarian collection.

Braikenridge was a man of retiring disposition, almost unknown in his home parish of Brislington. He retired from his firm at the early age of forty-six and spent the next thirty-six years filling his home (Broomwell House) with the largest collection of general and local antiquities in the West of England. He collected on a massive and indiscriminate scale and the disposal of the general collection was spread over eighty years, 1882–1962. In addition to the Somerset collection, Braikenridge bequeathed the Bristol and Gloucestershire collection to Bristol. Smyth-

DAVID COX

Lynmouth: the Sea Wall

Watercolour

BIRMINGHAM MUSEUMS AND
ART GALLERY

Pigott and Braikenridge died in 1853 and 1856 respectively, and with them the last vestige of Augustan influence. From then onwards antiquaries were motivated by Romanticism in the form of Gothic revival and its various offshoots.

David Cox O.W.S. (1783–1859), the famous Birmingham watercolour artist, came to the coast in 1821 and produced a typically competent watercolour of the sea wall at Lynmouth. The British Museum possesses a slight watercolour of the country road and Minehead beach, so it would not be unreasonable to assume that Cox spent some time exploring the coast and filling a sketch book before returning to his beloved Wales, no doubt using one of the many of the small coastal craft which plied across the Bristol Channel. Cox's son, David Cox Junior A.R.W.S. (1809–85), followed in his father's footsteps and visited Devon later in the century.

William Collins R.A. (1788–1847), the father of the author Wilkie Collins(1824–89) and Turner's associate, was a leading exponent of the early-Victorian narrative picture, producing a large number of genre scenes in addition to landscape paintings. Joshua Cristall P.O.W.S. (1767–1847) was a Cornishman of Scottish extraction whose father, a sea captain and merchant, had settled in Camborne. Largely self-taught, save for a short period at the Royal Academy Schools, his early style was similar to that of David Cox and Samuel Prout. After 1810 his work became somewhat sentimental. A much more talented artist to visit the

WILLIAM COLLINS

Fisherman

Watercolour 225 x 165mm

J. COLLINS AND SON, BIDEFORD

JOSHUA CRISTALL

Houses at Minehead 1811

Watercolour

BRITISH MUSEUM

JAMES HOLLAND

Lynmouth, Devon 22 August 1849

Watercolour

BRITISH MUSEUM

PETER DE WINT

Lynmouth, Devon
Winton Waterfall.

Watercolour and bodycolour
over pencil 620 x 450mm

BIRMINGHAM MUSEUMS AND
ART GALLERY

THOMAS LANDSEER

The Old Mill at Lynton

Watercolour

BRITISH MUSEUM

area was Peter De Wint O.W.S. (1784–1849) the son of a Dutch/American father and Scottish mother whose work is characterized by panoramic views executed with shallow broad washes.

Other painters active along the coast included Sir Edwin Landseer's brother, Thomas Landseer A.R.A. (1795–1880) and James Holland O.W.S. (1800–70). Landseer, like his brother, was a pupil of the Plymouth artist Benjamin Robert Haydon and a competent artist in his own right though most of his life was spent engraving his brother's work. Holland was born at Burslem, Staffordshire of a family of pottery painters and designers. He moved to London in 1819 and after a visit to France (1831) was influenced by the work of Richard Parkes Bonington (1802–28). The amateur, Thomas Brittain Vacher (1805–80) also painted on Exmoor at this time.

The period, 1770–1840, had been a fertile one for artists who had visited the coast and the Lyn Valley and had produced a considerable volume of work of varying aesthetic quality though all with a commercial and saleable value. Most of the great names of English watercolour painting came, stayed for a few days or weeks, and then moved on, in exactly the same way as the visitors who were their market. Some, like Daniell, Cox and Turner, had specific subject matter in mind; others, like De Wint, arrived on a speculative basis thinking that if London and Ilfracombe print sellers could market such a quantity of printed material, then they should be able to sell their pictures to the better type of visitor. This was, in fact, so and accounts for the spread of this type of artistic material throughout the country.

Chapter Four

NATURALISTIC
AND PICTURESQUE PAINTING
Mid to Late Nineteenth Century

With the accession to the throne of the young Queen Victoria, the country settled down to a period of relative prosperity, expansion and consolidation and, above all, becoming an imperial power. It was during this period that the so-called 'Victorian' influence came and went. Artistically this was the fragmentation and decline of the Romantic school. Turner was still very active. With his restless energy unaffected by old age, he was producing more paintings of a non-commercial type, preferring to concentrate on his own highly personal view of the world and anticipating the achievements of the French Impressionist painters later in the century. Lyrical Romanticism lingered in the painting of Constable and Girtin, though they were essentially naturalistic painters, striving to share their feelings about subject matter with viewers of their works.

It is worth noting that other than the great annual exhibitions in London (The Royal Academy and the Watercolour Society) no opportunity existed for the major part of the public to see paintings by leading artists except through a small band of active dealers. It was to overcome this problem that Turner had a private gallery incorporated into his home under the care of his father, the South Molton barber, for whom he had a great affection. Such was Turner's standing that the old man would appear to have been kept busy showing prospective purchasers of his son's work around the gallery and often selling paintings. One would suspect that many purchasers of the artist's steel engravings were determined to acquire an original work by the artist, though one wonders, looking at some of the Turner Collection in the Tate Gallery, what, given the prevailing tastes of the day, they would have made of the vast majority of Turner's late paintings. Turner left the contents of his studio (and gallery) to the nation on his death in 1851. These were mainly late paintings, unattractive to the buying public who would seem to have preferred the accomplished but dull pictures produced by the growing number of provincial and London painters. These artists exhibited in public halls, descendants of old Assembly Rooms like the Egyptian Hall in London or with the growing number of new art societies springing up in industrial cities like Bristol, Birmingham and Liverpool. Popular taste of the period is exemplified in collections left en masse to public galleries such as the Sheepshank collection in the Victoria & Albert Museum and the Nettlefold collection in the Birmingham Art Gallery.

As the century wore on the Romantic movement fragmented, degenerated and went into terminal decline though in its final moments some glorious works of art were produced. The movements which followed ranged from the Pre-Raphaelite Brotherhood to Augustus Welby Pugin's Gothic revival and produced everything from small paintings of popular, sentimental subjects to those with grand, historical themes depicting particularly scenes in ancient Greece and Rome and recent heroic events such as the Battle of Trafalgar and the victory at Waterloo.

Through all these shifts and changes of artistic fashion, the topographical movement held a relatively untroubled course, though very much the poor relation of both the major art boom and the grand and expensive painters of historical, allegorical and portrait works who filled the walls of the Royal

Academy. Even watercolour painters of landscapes and townscapes were not immune to the shifts of public taste and began to produce pictures in the grand manner imitating oil paintings, handsome to look at and beautifully framed. These were destined for the exhibitions of the Royal Academy and Old Watercolour Society, but nevertheless they have survived in many private collections and we can appreciate the achievements of these artists, despite the excessive use of body colour and gum-arabic to produce what is, in effect, a large and heavy watercolour.

In a further twist of artistic fashion and public taste, book and magazine illustration became popular with many artists. Advances in print technology provided for lavish illustration, albeit in black and white, of many books both fiction and non-fiction. At the same time, the monied public was, courtesy of Thomas Cook, travelling further and further afield and demanding pictures and prints of what it saw and artists soon followed in their footsteps. A good example of what an artist could do to reach and sell to this market is exemplified by the Scottish painter David Roberts R.A. (1796–1864). His earlier work consisted mainly of interior and exterior paintings of continental churches. He went to Egypt and the Levant in the late 1830s, producing sketches of Egyptian temples, Coptic and Orthodox churches and monasteries, together with many images of Islamic mosques. These were reproduced as lithographs and the originals formed the basis of highly successful exhibitions. As Turner before him, he exhibited and sold his original works and produced a number of fashionable folios of tinted lithographs from the original pictures. Edward Lear (1812–88) was another artist of this type who travelled extensively in the Levant and produced a vast number of line wash drawings which were as successful commercially as his limericks and are still highly regarded and sought after to this day.

The less adventuresome stayed at home and produced work which, via the medium of woodblock engraving, could be used to illustrate anything from the *Illustrated London News* and *Punch* to books extolling the beauty and virtues of popular tourist areas, including Exmoor. Given the movement away from Augustan order and Romantic feeling it was inevitable that naturalism would become the driving force for the majority of artists during the middle of the nineteenth century. Added to this was a sentimentality shown at its best in Sir Edwin Landseer's *The Old Shepherd's Chief Mourner* but which became all prevailing and an overwhelming force in the hands of lesser artists.

Until the coming of the railway, access to the heart of Exmoor was always difficult and slow and most artists like most visitors had confined their attentions to the coast and its hinterland. In 1855 the Reverend George Tugwell wrote *A North Devon Handbook,* illustrated by William Willis and published by Banfield and in the following year, written in the third person, *The North Devon Scenery Book* illustrated by H.B.Scougall. In the latter book, Tugwell's hero, Andrew Carnegie, travelled to

H.B. SCOUGALL

St Peter's, Combe Martin

Illustration in Rev. George Tugwell, *The North Devon Scenery Book,* Low, Simpkin Marshall, London and Banfield, Ilfracombe 1856

DEVON AND EXETER INSTITUTION, EXETER

H.B. SCOUGALL

Ilfracombe from Hillsborough

Illustration in Rev. George Tugwell, *The North Devon Scenery Book*, Low, Simpkin Marshall, London and Banfield, Ilfracombe 1856

DEVON AND EXETER INSTITUTION, EXETER

H.B. SCOUGALL

Simonsbath

Illustration in Rev. George Tugwell, *The North Devon Scenery Book* Low, Simpkin Marshall, London and Banfield, Ilfracombe 1856

DEVON AND EXETER INSTITUTION, EXETER

Exmoor by sea, boarding a ship for Lynmouth at the Cumberland Basin in Bristol. Whilst staying in Lynmouth he took the opportunity to go to Brendon via Watersmeet. The trip, in traditional manner, was accomplished on pony-back and Carnegie comments on the 'glorious view of undulating hill and woods stretching away to the sea'. Later that day the writer was overcome by a sense of loneliness. 'Whichever way he looked the view was the same, there was something awful in the endlessness of the view.'

Carnegie enjoyed fishing at Withypool and commented, 'Who would not exchange the din of Bristol, Babylon or leisure for the eternal quiet of beautiful Exmoor'. He then voiced the view that the best way to see Exmoor was to follow the River Barle, essentially a moorland stream, from its tributary near Mole's Chamber, through Simonsbath and Withypool, to Dulverton. This part of his journey was accomplished on foot. The book is, as one would expect from a Banfield publication, reasonably well illustrated by Scougall.

When in 1873 the Taunton–Dulverton–Barnstaple railway was opened, access to the southern and western sides of the moor became much easier. Passengers for the coast disembarked at Barnstaple and completed their journey in one of the many four-in-hand vehicles plying between Barnstaple, Ilfracombe and Lynton and Lynmouth. A year later the Taunton–Watchet–Minehead line was completed, serving the eastern and northern sides of the moor while the Barnstaple line was soon extended to Ilfracombe. It was also possible to reach Ilfracombe via the Southern Railway, rather than by using the services of the Great Western Railway. Finally, in 1885, the Exe Valley Line was opened linking Tiverton with Bampton, Dulverton and the northern end of the Exe Valley. The much loved and ridiculed narrow gauge line opened in 1898 between Barnstaple and Lynton was short-lived, closing in 1935.

With the railways came not only the commercial advantages of quick transportation of livestock and produce, but also, in season, a new generation of tourists. The prospering middle classes continued to visit the Bristol Channel resorts, but as the century wore on the introduction of cheap rail fares and the added inducement of a boat trip from Portishead, Bristol and South Wales to Ilfracombe and Minehead, was instrumental in attracting the newly emerging working classes to the area. This shift in the type of visitor, their tastes and the way they spent their money was ultimately to influence the type of picture being produced for sale.

At the turn of the century the type of visitor to the coast was neither as grand nor as affluent as in the previous fifty years. Reflecting the trend, a different type of artist arrived; an army of 'petit masters' who either worked in large industrial towns, supplying what was in effect wall covering for new middle class homes or illustrated books on history, topography and travel for consumption by the same market. The big artistic names did not come unless they had to.

In terms of Exmoor, the prime example of this genre was the Exeter artist, Frederick John Widgery (1861–1942), the son of William Widgery (1826–93). Widgery senior was born in North Molton and began his working life as a stone mason, moving to Exeter, where he painted copies of engravings before beginning to paint on his own account and subsequently producing large quantities of land- and seascapes and animal pictures. His colour sense was better than his son's, though both tend to be garish. Frederick John Widgery, a younger son, was educated at Exeter Cathedral School, Exeter School of Art, South Kensington and Antwerp. Returning to Devon, he settled down to a life producing work identical to his father's. His work is repetitive and at times he was a poor colourist but he could not paint enough Dartmoor and Exmoor scenes to meet public demand. His London agent was constantly asking for more. One wonders how he had time to become Lord Mayor of Exeter (1903–04) and a captain in the Volunteers in addition to illustrating many books such as Lady Northcote's *Devon* and John Presland's *Lynton and District*.

Walter Henry Sweet (1889–1943) was also born in Exeter and was educated at St John's School and the Exeter School of Art, becoming a competent watercolourist and etcher, producing moorland landscapes and coastal scenes. He worked successfully as a freelance artist, subsequently joining Valentine and Sons of Dundee as a postcard designer and commercial illustrator.

By the later nineteenth century groups of artists, mostly influenced by the 'Plein Air' school of painting in mainland Europe, began to settle in colonies on the English coast, seeking the hard bright light and ready supply of subject matter to be found in places such as Newlyn in Cornwall and Staithes in Yorkshire.

Exmoor failed to attract such a colony. The nearest Exmoor got to having a school of painters based on or near it during the nineteenth century was the small group of artists attracted to the West Country by the Taunton artist, John William North A.R.A., R.W.S. (1842–1924), a capable landscape painter in the popular tradition (a mixture of the Pre-Raphaelites and Corot). In the 1860s North discovered Halsway Manor in the Quantock Hills between Watchet and Crowcombe and used his discovery to tempt artist friends such as Frederick Walker A.R.A., O.W.S. (1840–75) and George John Pinwell (1842–75) to the area. It is, perhaps, surprising that no Somerset School of painting developed, but it was Frederick Walker, not North, who was the natural leader and he died at the relatively early age of thirty-five, having become an associate of the Royal Academy and a member of the Old Watercolour Society. The weather on and around Exmoor was not to the liking of the majority of artists: constant mist and rain were no substitute for hard bright sunshine and a relatively low rainfall. The colony did not materialise and North, while achieving a modest reputation both as a painter and illustrator, spent much of his life without any marked success attempting to produce an ideal artist's paper of high quality.

One interesting product of the declining Romantic movement was the

FREDERICK JOHN WIDGERY

Barnstaple Bridge and the River Taw

An illustration for Lady Rosalind Northcote's book, *Devon: Its Moorlands, Streams and Coasts* Chatto and Windus 1908

J. COLLINS AND SON, BIDEFORD

FREDERICK JOHN WIDGERY

The Moor near Brendon Two Gates

Illustration for John Presland's *Lynton and Lynmouth,* Chatto and Windus 1918

DEVON AND EXETER INSTITUTION, EXETER

FREDERICK JOHN WIDGERY

Dunkery Beacon

Watercolour 180 x 275mm

J. COLLINS AND SON, BIDEFORD

novel published by R.D. Blackmore in 1869, *Lorna Doone*, set on Exmoor in the closing years of the seventeenth century. It is a superb work of 'faction', skilfully blending historical facts and local folklore against a background suitably rearranged with considerable skill. Only the small church at Oare is immovable; hills become mountains, combes are gorges and waterfalls relocated. Blackmore, in his romance, made the Doones a gang of outlaws living with their leader, a nobleman of Scottish extraction at Badgworthy Water, a story current around North Devon in the author's time. It is a good tale which captures unerringly the character of the region, and gives a vivid picture of life as it must have been for those living a marginal existence in wild country with no effective form of law enforcement.

Whatever its origins, the tale has exerted a powerful influence on many who know of it, though have not necessarily read it, and it is a popular source of interest, drawing many to the moor to view the sights associated with the tale, particularly the church at Oare and the Doone Valley. It is somewhat ironic that the parishes of Culbone, Stoke Pero and Oare had a reputation of being singularly unattractive to any parson.

Another Exmoor example of the declining Romantic movement was the extension and alteration of Dunster Castle by Anthony Salvin (from 1867 onwards) to give the castle its highly picturesque, medieval appearance. In addition to work on the castle, George Fownes Luttrell

JOHN WILLIAM NORTH

Exford from the bridge

Illustration for Richard Jefferies' 'Summer in Somerset' in *English Illustrated Magazine* 1888

Opposite above

WALTER HENRY SWEET

Watersmeet, Lynmouth

Watercolour 170 x 350mm

J.COLLINS AND SON, BIDEFORD

Opposite below

WALTER HENRY SWEET

The Yarn Market, Dunster

Watercolour 185 x 240mm

J. COLLINS AND SON, BIDEFORD

(1826–1910) purchased Cleeve Abbey and its lands, repairing the building and beginning excavations as well as initiating the restoration of the parish churches at Dunster and Minehead.

With the Romantic movement all but dead and the Gothic revival entering its final phase, William Burges (1827–81) designed Knightshayes Court near Tiverton for Sir John Heathcoat-Amory. A superb building aesthetically, it was also a temple of venery, serving as kennels for the family staghounds and including in the formal gardens a splendid topiary hedge of hounds chasing the fox, a rare combination. The final fling of the Gothic revival on Exmoor was a spate of church restoration (e.g. Winsford 1891 and Withypool 1901) which gave the moorland churches their current appearance.

Since the reintroduction of stag hunting on Exmoor in 1855, the shooting of stags largely ceased, and were a man to be seen shooting a stag he could be ostracised. The deer did as much damage as ever, but through the goodwill of upland farmers stag hunting was finally established as a method of management and conservation. Upland farmers were coerced or wooed to share the compelling excitement of the chase and compensated for damage caused by feeding stags. Landlords expected their tenants to allow the hunt to have access to their farms. All classes of society would attend a meet and enjoy the chase on horseback. Cecil Aldin records that at the turn of the century there was not a single tradesman in Porlock who did not hunt. Gradually middle and upper class sportsmen started to visit the moor itself, in contrast to the coastal holiday-makers, making for Porlock or one of the smaller northern villages. Although earlier visitors like Wordsworth, Coleridge and Tennyson had visited Dulverton it was the sportsmen who opened up the uplands for today's visitors – whatever their interest.

In addition to the staghounds, several packs of foxhounds hunted over the moor. Foxes have always been abundant in the upland country and during the eighteenth and early nineteenth century private packs were brought to the moor to enjoy the chase. Parson Jack Russell, of Swimbridge, and Parson John Froude, of Knowstone and Molland, both hunted much on Exmoor with foxhounds and also harriers. Late in the nineteenth century Nicholas Snow, the Squire of Oare, kept a fine pack of foxhounds at his manor house, the famous Stars of the West, the forerunners of today's Exmoor Foxhounds.

One of the people who popularised staghunting was Parson Jack Russell. The Reverend John Russell (1795–1883) was rector of Swimbridge, a man highly regarded by all, and having friends at all levels of society. His enduring memorial, in addition to the moral influence he exerted during his forty-five year ministry on Exmoor, is the terrier which bears his name. Russell was born at Dartmouth, and educated at Blundell's School, Tiverton and Oxford, before taking holy orders. While at Oxford he bought a terrier 'Trump', as the foundation stock on which he based his own type of terrier. During his long life he perfected that type, but never sold a puppy: he always gave them as gifts. In Russell's time, North Devon was renowned for its working terriers and the Parson added to that reputation by developing a type which was to become world famous. One indication of the Jack Russell's popularity is that hardly any group photograph, whatever the occasion or class of society it depicts, taken in North Devon before the First World War, is without the terrier in the near central position. It was beloved by school children and dowager duchesses alike.

One of the features of Parson Russell's ministry was his friendship with Albert Edward, Prince of Wales. It was this friendship which brought the Prince to Exmoor to hunt in August 1879. The Royal approbation of the Devon and Somerset Staghounds was dramatic in its effect. It put stag hunting and Exmoor on the map. Hunting people flocked to the moor, accommodation and horses were provided and soon a thriving local industry was established, which in due course had profound artistic consequences.

The leading West Country artist of the period, meanwhile, was Frederick Richard Lee R.A. (1794–1879). Born at Barnstaple, he joined the army during the Napoleonic Wars and subsequently entered the Royal Academy Schools in 1818, becoming an Associate in 1834 and a

FREDERICK RICHARD LEE

Devonshire Scenery 1842

Oil on canvas 1168 x 1524mm

RICHARD GREEN, LONDON

FREDERICK RICHARD
LEE

On the Edge of Exmoor 1842

Oil on canvas 1270 x 940mm

SOTHEBY'S, SUSSEX

Full Member in 1838. Lee was a painter of coastal scenes and river or
woodland landscape. He lived in Devon where he found much of his
subject matter but used his yacht to explore the coasts of France, Spain
and Italy. He retired in 1870 and died in South Africa while visiting his
family. Another West Country man to produce a large volume of material
of the area was Arthur Wild Parsons (1854–1931). He was a Bristolian
through and through. His father was a doctor in the city and Parsons
studied locally and remained in Redlands for the rest of his life.
Throughout his life he painted the Bristol Docks and the Bristol
Channel, though when his brother became vicar of a Cornish parish, he
extended his field of operations to Cornwall. His only visit to mainland
Europe was to Venice and he subsequently produced a large number of
Venetian subjects. As a painter he was much more interested in the
Exmoor coastline than in the moor itself.

Another Bristolian was William James Muller (1812–45) who, if he had not died young, at the age of thirty-two, might have become one of the period's leading artists. The son of a German immigrant who became Curator of the British Museum, Muller was apprenticed to J.B. Pyne and in 1833 became a founder member of the Bristol Sketch Club. He stayed in the city until 1838 when he left to travel in Greece and Egypt at the same time as David Roberts. He also followed the popular tourist routes to France, Holland, Germany and Venice in search of material which would be attractive to the rich families who now flocked to the continent. Shortly before his death of a heart attack he visited the North Devon and Somerset coast (1844) and produced a series of highly attractive watercolours. Writing from Lynmouth in August of that year he noted that 'Here I am painting away. This week have had rain, wind &c, so I am doing little; but however disagreeable, I must keep to it three or four weeks longer.'

WILLIAM JAMES MULLER

Rocky Stream and Ravine, Lynmouth 1844

Oil on canvas 865 x 660mm

LAWRENCE FINE ART, CREWKERNE

WILLIAM JAMES MULLER

Lynton 1844

Watercolour

BRITISH MUSEUM

WILLIAM JAMES MULLER

Lynmouth: Sunlit Cliffs 1844

Watercolour

A typical late work

BRITISH MUSEUM

ALBERT GOODWIN

Combe Martin

Watercolour, pencil and
bodycolour 255 x 355mm

SOTHEBY'S, SUSSEX

Albert Goodwin R.W.S. (1845–1932) whose work is currently enjoying renewed popularity, lived at Ilfracombe for a time while his brother Harry, who painted in a more sentimental and less accomplished fashion, lived and died in Torquay. Albert studied under the Pre-Raphaelite painters, Arthur Hughes (1832–1915) and Ford Madox Brown (1812–93). He was an ardent admirer of Turner, visited Italy with Ruskin and also travelled widely in Europe, India and the South Seas. He paid great attention to the effects of atmosphere and light and this is particularly evident in his paintings of the North Devon coast.

ALBERT GOODWIN

Combe Martin 1882

Watercolour
250 x350mm

J. COLLINS AND SON, BIDEFORD

The Cornishman, Charles Edward Brittan (1837–88), and his son (born 1870), both held the same name and both painted in North Devon. Brittan Junior lived at Lewdown on Dartmoor and illustrated an edition of *Lorna Doone* in 1911 and Alfred Vowles' *The Lorna Doone Country*, 1925. He exhibited regularly at the Royal Academy and had a one-man show at the Ackermann Galleries. Some of his pictures were bought by Queen Mary and by the Prince of Wales, later the Duke of Windsor.

CHARLES EDWARD
BRITTAN

Moorland River

Watercolour

J. COLLINS AND SON, BIDEFORD

CHARLES EDWARD
BRITTAN

*Rugged Coast with
Fisherman*

Watercolour 315 x 490mm

J. COLLINS AND SON, BIDEFORD

JOHN WHITE

Bringing in the Flock

Watercolour 100 x 305mm

J. COLLINS AND SON, BIDEFORD

Another painter to settle in Devon was the Scot, John White R.I., R.O.I. (1851–1933). Born in Edinburgh, he was educated in Australia, his parents having emigrated, but he returned to England to study painting and settled in Beer on the South Devon coast. He was a leading exponent of the 'cottage gate' type of painting, presenting rural cottages in an inviting and sentimental manner, completely overlooking the fact that they were often wretched hovels and their occupants exploited and living in poverty. His pictures were, and are again (after falling from favour), highly regarded.

ALFRED ROBERT QUINTON

Bossington

Illustration for Ditchfield, *Cottage and Village Life in Rural England*, J.M.Dent 1912

DEVON AND EXETER INSTITUTION, EXETER

Another painter of this type was Alfred Robert Quinton (1853–1934) the acme of whose art can be found in his illustrations to Ditchfield's *Cottage and Village Life in Rural England*, 1912. This sumptuous and

ALFRED ROBERT QUINTON

Dunster Cottages

Illustration for Ditchfield, *Cottage and Village Life in Rural England,*
J.M.Dent 1912

DEVON AND EXETER INSTITUTION, EXETER

pretentious volume was aimed at the urban middle-class market and gave an idyllic view of rural squalor. Quinton did a wonderful job with the illustrations and then returned to his career of producing 'cottage gate' images for picture postcards, including some Exmoor scenes, and exhibiting rural watercolours at the Royal Academy. Beatrice Parsons (1870–1955), whilst an established portrait and landscape painter, rather overdid the 'rural idyll' in her watercolour of *The Terrace Garden, Porlock Bay.*

In 1890 Seeley and Co. published John Lloyd Warden Page's *An Exploration of Exmoor and the Hill Country of West Somerset,* illustrated by a series of high quality wood-block engravings from pen and ink drawings by Alfred Dawson (fl. 1860–93), a London-based landscape

BEATRICE E. PARSONS

The Terrace Garden, Porlock Bay

Watercolour 240 x 290mm

SOTHEBY'S, LONDON

ALFRED DAWSON

Culbone Church

Illustration for John Lloyd Warden Page, *An Exploration of Exmoor and the Hill Country of West Somerset,* Seeley & Co. 1890

DEVON AND EXETER INSTITUTION, EXETER

ALFRED DAWSON

Porlock Weir

Illustration for John Lloyd
Warden Page,
*An Exploration of Exmoor
and the Hill Country of
West Somerset,*
Seeley & Co. 1890

DEVON AND EXETER
INSTITUTION, EXETER

ALFRED DAWSON

Badgworthy Waterslide

Illustration for John Lloyd
Warden Page,
*An Exploration of Exmoor
and the Hill Country of
West Somerset,*
Seeley & Co. 1890

DEVON AND EXETER
INSTITUTION, EXETER

ALFRED DAWSON

Landacre Bridge

Illustration for John Lloyd Warden Page,
An Exploration of Exmoor and the Hill Country of West Somerset, Seeley & Co. 1890

DEVON AND EXETER INSTITUTION, EXETER

WILLIAM HENRY PIKE

*The Rhenish Tower,
Lynmouth*

Oil on canvas

MUSEUM OF NORTH DEVON,
BARNSTAPLE

HENRY GASTINEAU

Near the Waters Meet, Lynton, N.Devon

Watercolour and bodycolour over pencil 620 x 925mm

BIRMINGHAM MUSEUMS AND ART GALLERY

painter and etcher, and a worthy successor to Frederick Christian Lewis' *Scenery of the River Exe*, 1827.

An earlier artist whose style remained rooted in the 1820s was Henry G. Gastineau O.W.S. (1791–1876). A landscape and topographical watercolourist, he travelled widely in the British Isles, Switzerland and Italy. In 1829 he built a house in South London where he lived for the rest of his life, establishing a practice as a drawing master, producing a prolific number of topographical watercolours in a very dated and laboured style, and exhibiting regularly for almost fifty years. Of his range of material one could travel the British Isles and say, 'Gastineau has been here.' He loved painting the wild scenery of the Cornish and Devon coasts and achieved some of his best results in those parts.

Other artists working in the Exmoor area during the second half of the nineteenth century included the Plymouth landscape painter, William Henry Pike R.B.A. (1846–1908); the Dorking rustic genre painter, Charles Collins R.B.A. (fl.1867–1903) and the talented John William Schofield (fl.1899–1944) who studied in Paris under Bouguereau and produced many quality landscapes of subjects in and around Combe Martin and Lynton, two of the villages in which he lived. The Yorkshireman Edward Henry Holder (fl.1864–1917) also paid a visit, probably before an extended trip to South Africa.

The closing years of the nineteenth century marked a change of emphasis in painting on Exmoor. Until then the landscape itself and its interpretation had provided both the subject matter and the inspiration for the many artists who visited the area. The twentieth century was to see another style of painting develop on the moor; that of the sporting artist.

Opposite above

JOHN WILLIAM SCHOFIELD

The Rhenish Tower, Lynmouth 1899

Watercolour 255 x 355mm

J. COLLINS AND SON, BIDEFORD

Opposite below

EDWARD HENRY HOLDER

A Coastal Scene

Oil on canvas 1245 x 1880mm

SOTHEBY'S, SUSSEX

CHAPTER FIVE

SPORTING
AND OTHER PAINTERS
The Twentieth Century

Sporting art is one of the oldest of artistic genres though today, in line with the deprecation of field sports, it is not considered 'politically correct' either to be a practitioner or to take an interest in this genre. In artistic terms it is regarded by progressive thinkers as making the unacceptable acceptable, giving an attractive public image to an unattractive pastime!

On Exmoor hunting, and the hunting of the native red deer in particular, is part of the traditional culture of the moor and, time without memory, has played a vital part in moor life. As we have seen the red deer were almost exterminated during the early nineteenth century until the Devon and Somerset Staghounds were formed in 1855 with the object of saving them from extinction by organising venery rather than allowing free-for-all killing. Today this might seem rather odd and not a little paradoxical, yet the mid-nineteenth century saw many idealistic enterprises to help the less well off. A good example was the establishment, in London, by a group of earnest evangelical Christians, of what is now a national brewery: to give the poor 'good English ale' at a low price, to offset the effect of cheap, easily available spirits (gin) – 'drunk for a penny, dead drunk for twopence'. Exactly the same principle applied. The desire to do good strongly outweighed the problem which was being tackled and the end justified the means. In the case of Exmoor, the conservation of the red deer: in London, drunkenness and its attendant problems. Today, when historical moral values are being challenged on all sides, Parson Jack Russell, rector of Swimbridge and friend of the Prince of Wales, who had a reputation for the highest moral rectitude, would certainly have regarded hunting, in all its forms, as a God-given right of man's dominion over all animals. He would also have detested illegitimacy. Today progressive thought takes exactly the opposite view: hunting in any form is totally unacceptable, illegitimate children are now perfectly acceptable.

Sporting illustrations began to cover the pages of contemporary Exmoor books, from H.B. Hall's *Exmoor: or In the Footsteps of St Hubert*, 1849, to F.J. Snell's *Book of Exmoor*, 1903, via *Ward Lock's Guide* of 1890. Yet while many serious sporting artists went to the spiritual home of the Romantic cult, Scotland, none bothered to visit Exmoor – those members of the hunting world making their way to Exmoor had, until the 1890s, to make do with very third-rate and unattractive visual images of Exmoor and stag hunting in the form of poor quality steel engravings and lithographs – mainly as book illustrations.

With the coming of the railways the journey to Exmoor had become comparatively easy and in 1906 the opening of a line from Westbury to Taunton so avoiding Bristol, reduced the journey time from Paddington to a little under five hours. Not only was this popular with holiday-makers, but with the Exmoor hunting season running from the 1 August to 30 April, the new line soon attracted considerable interest among the London-based hunting fraternity who travelled to Exmoor to hunt taking their horses with them. At the turn of the century and well into the twentieth century it was a common sight, at both Paddington and Euston, to see hunters waiting to be boxed for the journeys to

Exmoor and Leicestershire respectively. Cecil Aldin in 1932 was the first to depict the presence of motor cars on the Exmoor uplands followed, in 1938, by his fellow sporting artist Michael Lyne.

Possibly the first recognised sporting artist to work on Exmoor during the two final decades of the nineteenth century was Frederick Hall R.B.C., N.E.A.C. (1860–1948) who painted at Porlock in the late 1880s whilst a member of the Newlyn School (1885–97). His paintings range from 'plein-air' studies of impressionistic landscapes in warm glowing colours to sporting genre of which *The Meet at Porlock* is an excellent example.

Allen Culpeper Sealy (1850–1927) is a little-known artist whose most familiar work is a set of four prints of the Duke of Beaufort's foxhounds, entitled *A Day with the Blue and Buffs* published in the 1890s. About the same time Sealy published a set of four sepia photogravures of *A Day with the Devon and Somerset Staghounds*. These are rare but some still survive in Exmoor homes. Thomas Blinks, (1853–1910) who was the master at depicting hounds at work, worked on Exmoor uplands during the 1890s and produced many fine paintings.

Hard on the heels of Sealy and Blinks came Robert Polhill Bevan (1865–1925), a strange, enigmatic character, who lived at Hawkridge from 1895 to 1897 in order to hunt on Exmoor. Bevan was born at Hove, Sussex, of Welsh Quaker stock and made a leisurely entry into the painting profession via Winchester, the Westminster School of Art and Julian's in Paris. It was this same *atelier* in the *rue de Dragon* which another young English artist, Alfred Munnings, attended in 1902 and 1903.

Enjoying a small private income gave Bevan a freedom not shared by his contemporaries. Neither was his subject matter – horses. It is not possible to determine exactly when his equestrian obsession began but it may have been at the age of twenty-seven when (after visiting Spain to study Velazquez and Goya) he went to Tangier and painted with the 'Glasgow Boy' Joseph Crawhall (1861–1913) and the Punch sporting artist George Denholm Armour (1864–1949) both members of the so-called 'sporting set'. Armour, in his memoirs, relates that the Tangier hunt consisted of some 12 to 14 couple of hounds drafted from England and Wales who

FREDERICK HALL

The Meet at Porlock 1905

Oil on canvas 560 x 445mm

PHILLIPS, FINE ART
AUCTIONEERS, BATH

ROBERT POLHILL BEVAN

Huntsman and Hounds

Lithograph 185 x 145mm

Front cover for a portfolio of four hunting scenes 1898

ROYAL ALBERT MEMORIAL MUSEUM, EXETER

hunted well. Crawhall acted as First Whip and Armour as Second Whip, subsequently becoming Master for a season following the resignation of the Duke of Frias. Crawhall, as well as being a superb painter, was a natural horseman and no mean jockey.

From Tangier Bevan moved, somewhat surprisingly, to Pont Aven in Brittany where he was to paint with Gauguin for a couple of years. Paul Gauguin (1848–1903) was, by any standard, a bizarre character. Originally a Paris stockbroker and Sunday painter, he deserted his wife and went to live in Pont Aven, between 1886–90, and had a disastrous stay of two months with Vincent Van Gogh in Arles, Provence. In 1891 he went to Tahiti, only to return to France in 1893, poverty stricken and looking for money. He subsequently made his way back to his old Brittany haunts and there joined forces with Bevan, returning to the South Sea Islands in 1895. Gauguin's health was always frail and he had been seriously hurt in a brawl with sailors in Brittany during 1894. He died in 1903 in Tahiti, having 'gone bush'. When they parted company in 1895, Bevan made his way to Hawkridge on Exmoor, an interesting move given the background of the man and his recent past which included meeting Renoir and seeing the work of Cézanne for the first time.

Gauguin left his mark on Bevan's painting, but while the foundation of his technique and attitude to painting was firmly laid under Gauguin's influence, two years hunting and painting on Exmoor gave full reign to his equestrian inclination and it is a source of regret that few paintings of this period survive. A handful of extant lithographs, drawings and watercolours give some indication of the paradoxical nature and essential Englishness of Bevan's art together with the charismatic influence of Gauguin which was to become so evident in Bevan's later paintings of London cabyards and horse sales.

In the years after leaving Exmoor Bevan was a familiar figure at the commercial end of the London equestrian scene in his narrow-brimmed bowler hat and three-quarter length riding coat, indistinguishable from the owners, copers, knackers and grooms busily engaged around him as he worked. His work is in the Tate Gallery (Chantrey Purchase) and in 1956 the Tate held a retrospective exhibition.

It is difficult to say how and why Cecil Charles Windsor Aldin R.B.A. (1870–1935) came to Exmoor. He could, as a rising young illustrator, have heard of Exmoor from a hunting acquaintance or from fellow artist John Charlton (1849–1917), who produced Devon and Somerset Staghounds' drawings when he and Aldin were working on the *Illustrated London News*. Alternatively he might have been introduced to the moor by his friend Sir Francis (Frank) Carruthers Gould R.B.A. (1844–1925), a

ROBERT POLHILL BEVAN

The Smithy Barn, Bolham, Tiverton

Lithograph

ASHMOLEAN MUSEUM, OXFORD

political cartoonist for the *Pall Mall Gazette* and other periodicals who was born in Barnstaple and, on retirement, settled in Porlock. Aldin was certainly hunting on Exmoor when Robert Sanders (Lord Bayford) was Master of the Devon and Somerset Staghounds, and the Squire of Oare, Nicholas Snow, was still hunting his famous pack of foxhounds, The Stars of the West, a reminder of the days when a squire had his own pack and kennels and hunted over his own land, though in Snow's case it would have been over Knight and Fortescue land. John Hassall produced a nice watercolour portrait of his friend, Aldin, at this time.

The young London artist was captivated and began a lifelong love affair with Exmoor. Initially he stayed at an old farmhouse at Alcombe Cross, then a hamlet near Minehead. Aldin commented that in 1930, 'the old farm had survived, but was surrounded by rows of modern houses and a shopping parade'. In those early years Aldin made use of the Beach Hotel at Minehead, its greatest virtue being that it had adequate stabling for horses, but it was not a good hunting centre, although located at the rail-head and did not require a four-in-hand ride to Porlock. Aldin liked the hotel which in the 1890s appeared old-

ROBERT POLHILL BEVAN

Barns in Somerset

Watercolour

This watercolour has been 'squared-off' by the artist
for transfer to a larger working surface: possibly canvas

BRITISH MUSEUM

fashioned though built only twenty years earlier. Perhaps he saw in it some of the merits of the old coaching inns which were one of his enduring passions. Describing the hotel in affectionate terms in *Exmoor, The Riding Playground of England,* he commented that 'it still retained the cruet and condiment habit'. From Aldin, that was a high standard of praise.

Subsequently Aldin transferred his loyalty to the Anchor at Porlock Weir. Porlock had become something of a Piccadilly Circus for hunting people who held the inn in high regard. In the 1890s the Anchor was owned and managed by John Goddard, one of England's finest innkeepers, a great sportsman, character and stag hunter. The fame of his inn was such that he could pick and choose his guests, and unless one was accepted by Goddard, it was impossible to stay there. It was, in effect, a private clubhouse for the hunting fraternity with three private sitting rooms, ten or twelve bedrooms and one bathroom. It had little to offer in the way of comfort by today's standards but had a wonderful

JOHN HASSALL

The Young Aldin at Work

Watercolour

ROY HERON

CECIL ALDIN

Study for Cloutsham Farm, Exmoor August 1925

The picture shows S.V. Hine pointing out to Miss Milrain the Huntsman and tufters drawing the combe above Home Water. Aldin rarely used oil on canvas.

Oil on canvas 470 x 605mm

SPINK AND SON, LONDON

host, lively minded guests and enormous stabling. One is tempted to wonder how so many gentlemen and their ladies coped with the demands on a single bathroom, after a hard and wet day's hunting! Aldin commented, 'Every year when I travelled to Porlock, it seemed more like going home than anything else – that is the charm of one's favourite Inn where the same band of sportsmen from all over England gathered every year from August to October.' A gentleman's club indeed.

After Goddard's death and a change in management at the Anchor, Aldin moved from Porlock Weir to Cloutsham Farm above Horner Woods and subsequently to various other houses. Although he moved his headquarters, one thing always delighted Aldin: the golden harvest moon rising over Hurlstone Point. To Aldin one of the many joys of Exmoor was the continued use of four-in-hand coaches as a means of transport. The four-in-hands plied between Minehead and Lynton and would drop the Anchor guests at Porlock to be collected by Goddard's private omnibus, a pair-horse affair. From his teens Aldin had always been besotted with coaching days and coaching ways. This gave rise to a series of six coaching prints in 1903, with a further set in the 1920s, supplemented by his book *Romance of the Road* and several books and print series on abbeys, cathedrals and manor houses, all to be seen on the old coaching routes and taken from the old roadbooks such as *Paterson's*. Alas for Aldin, the coaches had been replaced by motor buses by the 1920s.

As a requiem for the Anchor and its former owner, Aldin painted the inn from the quay on the first night that electric lighting was used, a labour of love and a tribute. Times changed, Goddard was gone, and so too had the ceremony of being 'played in' by the Porlock brass band on the green outside the inn during dinner – a traditional welcome to Aldin, such was the esteem in which he was held by the local population. About this time Aldin produced an article for *English Life* giving a fascinating account of sporting life on Exmoor.

It was Aldin's habit to spend either the spring and early summer on Exmoor or, alternatively, August and the first two weeks in September, when he could slip away from London without his wife and children during the early years of his married life, or in later life when he had his grandchildren with him. Aldin always took horses, dogs and personal chattels with him to help the party integrate into the Somerset scene. The death of his son, Dudley, in action during the First World War, was a devastating blow from which he never recovered. While it is true to say that he was not a broken man, that, and increasing health problems, made him channel what was left of his former legendary love of life into two new fields, dogs and children.

Dogs had always appeared in his work, indeed a cur dog or foxhound was the hallmark of an Aldin picture and, as the 1920s progressed, he gradually eased out of hunting and coaching subject matter in favour of canine material. At the end of his life he was producing almost

The Devon and Somerset

An illustrated article in *English Life* by Cecil Aldin

CECIL ALDIN

A Polo match on Dunster Lawns 1924

Coloured chalks

ROY HERON

CECIL ALDIN

The Anchor, Porlock Weir

On the night that electric light was first used at the hotel
Photolithographic print, published by Heinemann 1921

BURLINGTON GALLERY, LONDON

exclusively dog material, particularly etchings, which, with his increasing arthritis, became the only media that he could manage. Having lost a much-loved son, Aldin became absorbed with his daughter's children and the children of his Exmoor friends. He was always an innovator, both in his work as a sporting artist and in whatever else he did. As a remount officer in the First World War, he was the first to use women as stable grooms and succeeded in having an all-women depot in his Berkshire remount stables, until the arrival of Alfred Munnings to serve as his assistant.

During August 1903, an enthusiastic female artist appeared on Exmoor, Lucy Kemp-Welch R.B.A. (1869–1958). She was the guest of Lord Fortescue at Castle Hill, had recently been elected to membership of the Royal Society of British Artists and was soon to purchase the School of Art at Bushey in Hertfordshire. During her visit she produced a series of stag head studies and on a later visit (1908), a large oil of the type which were to make her famous. Though comparable in size, the Exmoor oil *For Life* lacks the visual impact of *Colt Hunting in the New Forest* and the First World War *Forward the Guns*. Superbly crafted, they are now in the Tate Gallery (Chantrey Bequest).

Lucy Kemp-Welch, and later, Sir Alfred Munnings and Lionel Edwards were drawn to the moorland by the same vast, empty landscapes which attracted Aldin who observed, 'On the greater part of

CECIL ALDIN

The Devon and Somerset Staghounds at Badgworthy Water

Photolithographic print, published by Alfred Bell

BURLINGTON GALLERY, LONDON

CECIL ALDIN

A Scottie and a Westie

Dry point etching

HEALE GALLERY, SOMERSET

Exmoor not a house can be seen, even from the highest altitudes, it is the land of the horseman and walker, but for the scarcity of landmarks – most of which are only distinguishable to a man of Exmoor.' Such remoteness greatly appealed to Aldin and his fellow sporting artists and this, together with the sport which they enjoyed and the friendships with Exmoor people, tied them to the moor in a way that no earlier artists had been tied.

Previous artists had been voyeurs, observers, with an eye to commercial potential. The group of sporting artists, then emerging, were committed to Exmoor people and institutions. They absorbed the culture and ethos of the moor. For them the wide open moorland acres cried out for a hunt to cross them, as the most natural thing in the world. Their attachment to the moor and to its people suggests that if there were ever an Exmoor school of painters it was made up of these artists, their associates and followers. They might not be permanent residents and they might not paint the day-to-day back-breaking work of moor people, as did the members of the Newlyn School in Cornwall, but it was they more than anyone, either before or since, who totally absorbed the moor, and transmitted this love in their work to a wide public, not necessarily of sporting inclination.

The three major members of the group were Cecil Aldin, Alfred Munnings and Lionel Edwards. Cecil Aldin was the senior (being eight years older than both Munnings and Edwards, each born in 1878) and a successful artist while Munnings was still studying in Paris (1902–03) and Edwards, attempting to consolidate his position as an emerging sporting artist, producing Aldin pastiches, sometimes in collaboration with Lance Thackery (d.1916). So successful was Aldin that plagiarising was a major problem for him in the United Kingdom, the United States and France, though in fairness, Aldin himself leant heavily on the ideas and inspiration generated by the work of Major Godfrey Douglas Giles (1857–1941). Giles produced a number of paintings of military engagements taken from what was, in effect, an aerial position. He later incorporated these ideas into a series of paintings of hunting countries giving rise to the birth of the modern sporting painting.

Other than age, the great difference between Aldin and the other two men was the influence of French impressionism. Aldin always remained at heart a man of the 1890s, illustrating and painting in the stylised manner of the incomparable Randolph Caldecott (1846–86) and drawing in the classical mould of *Punch* artists and *Yellow Book* contributors. Munnings however, would have seen the work of the French impressionists during his stay in Paris and immediately started to alter his tonal values and brushwork to reflect their simple vibrant colours and free brushwork. Edwards did not reflect these changes until the early 1920s when he evolved a highly personal and very commercial style that was never to change until age coarsened his brushwork and reduced the tones of his colouring.

Sporting art has never been cheap and in 1901, with the accession of

Edward VII to the throne, equestrian and sporting painting became fashionable – the King's enthusiasm for racing and hunting ensuring Royal patronage and where the King went, so did a large number of his subjects. Demand for sporting material was insatiable and prices good. Aldin was a beneficiary of this revival and as an illustrator always saw to it that his subject was in the foreground of any painting – the first prerequisite of a successful print, and Aldin was very successful indeed.

Munnings returned to England in 1904 and took the first steps towards becoming the President of the Royal Academy (1944–49), working initially in East Anglia, both from a studio and a gypsy caravan. In 1911 he moved to Lamorna Cove, a few miles from Newlyn, developing a style which after the First World War was to give him international fame and guarantee a substantial income.

Edwards in the early 1920s made a determined effort to drop his pre-war style with its heavy reliance on Aldin's work and create a working style which would be both light and fresh, correct in detail, pleasing in demeanour and which would combine his knowledge of horses and hunting with atmospheric landscape painting. He was so successful that he became the darling of the hunting fraternity in the 1920s and '30s, producing an endless stream of opaque watercolours of hunts throughout the British Isles. He effectively reduced the principles of impressionism to a format which would give a 'Lionel Edwards sky', the field in the middle distance and some action in the foreground. In this he and other sporting artists were helped considerably by the availability of wide angle photographs in magazines such as *The Field* and *The Sporting & Dramatic News*, which provided a fund of reference material. Edwards also spent much time following hunts so that Cecil Aldin, in the early 1920s, complained about 'that chap Edwards'

LUCY KEMP-WELCH

For Life, Exmoor

Oil on canvas
3050 x 1525mm

Exhibited at the
Royal Academy 1908

DEVON AND EXETER
INSTITUTION, EXETER

LUCY KEMP-WELCH

Ponies on the Moor

Oil on canvas 120 x 220mm

DEVON AND EXETER
INSTITUTION, EXETER

following him around the countryside during his own hunting expeditions.

Exmoor was the ideal habitat for these men. It was a form of escape for those who wished to quit London. Each could indulge his passion for hunting and at the same time paint and make contact with potential clients, for, by the early 1920s, the rich and famous in the hunting world were visiting the moor in ever-increasing numbers for at least one month during the season. It was an ideal situation for any artist and one which offset the popular tourist culture of the coastal towns, ensuring a regular stream of visitors, comparable with those who first visited the area a hundred or so years previously.

Sir Alfred Munnings first visited the moor in 1911, perhaps on a visit from his Cornish base at Lamorna, and made drawings of the Devon and Somerset Staghounds for future reference. Munnings continued to work on paintings of Cornish packs and among the works of this period can be numbered the fine tempera painting *Ned on the Brown Mare,* shown at Munnings' first exhibition at the Leicester Galleries, London, in 1913. It was immediately sold to the gallery owner for forty guineas (£42) plus a copyright fee of twenty guineas (£21).

In contrast Lionel Edwards came to Exmoor early, taken by his mother to Lynton for a brief holiday in the 1890s. He had his first sight of red deer from the little railway that ran between Barnstaple and Lynton and his first experience of hunting with the Devon and Somerset. It was a disaster, both horse and rider falling over the parapet of a bridge. However, the mishap gave him an introduction to moor people for he spent the night at the Bawdens' Farm at Hawkridge, and was guided home over 'a vast stretch of treeless country by a small boy, Ernest Bawden, later to become a famous huntsman of the D. & S.'.

In 1902 Edwards returned to Exmoor in company with his elder brother who was on leave from the army. Taking two horses with them, they hunted and hacked over the moor until Edwards knew every hill and combe and came to love the country more than anywhere in

ALFRED MUNNINGS

The Artist at Work

Pencil drawing, signed and inscribed

SPINK AND SON, LONDON

ALFRED MUNNINGS

*Sidney Tucker (Huntsman)
and Ernest Bawden (Whip)
bringing hounds down
Cloutsham Combe 1916*

Watercolour and gouache
410 x 515mm

SOTHEBY'S, LONDON

England. During this visit, Edwards hired the old Porlock parish room, having quickly sold his first stag-hunting picture of *A Kill at Horner Mill*. The parish room was in fact something of a venue for artists requiring a studio (including Aldin) or wishing to sell their work, and, on his first showing, Lionel Edwards sold out. An encouraging situation for a young and struggling artist. In addition to the parish room, Porlock boasted another sporting art exhibition to be found in the shop of Mr Perkins, the tailor, who was famous not only for his riding breeches, but also for the sporting pictures which he sold as a sideline.

It was Edwards' habit throughout his life to visit Exmoor at least once a year, more often if he could manage it, both to hunt with the Devon and Somerset Staghounds and to paint. His wife never wanted to leave home, but she always made an exception with the visit to Exmoor which she thoroughly enjoyed, together with hunting alongside her husband. Sir Alfred Munnings advised her that 'if she wished to see stag hunting, she should always endeavour to be in at the death – since this was what hunting was all about'. Hunting was Edwards' life; he in fact hunted with 91 packs of foxhounds and at eighty was still jumping gates.

During the First World War whilst Lionel Edwards and Cecil Aldin were working as remount officers with the rank of Major, Munnings, due to blindness in his right eye following an accident, was sidelined in Cornwall and engaged in painting horse fairs, gypsy encampments, hop pickers and landscapes. However, he too was determined to become a remount officer and go to France. Just how he managed it varies with the source of information on the subject, but what is certain is that he joined Cecil Aldin at his Calcot Park Remount Depot near Reading and spent the whole of 1917 working as Aldin's assistant. This move was the start of a train of events which ultimately took Munnings to the top of his profession, though, at the time, he only wanted to get to France and the front line. Through his work at the Remount Depot, Munnings became acquainted with the Canadian Calvary, shortly to embark for France. He seized the opportunity and had himself appointed an official War Artist to go with the cavalry to their French quarters and on to the front line. This was to be a watershed in his career. When the pictures of the Canadian troops were exhibited at the Royal Academy in 1919 they caused great public interest.

Among the paintings was one which, more than any other, was to shape Munnings' future; a portrait of General Jack Seely (later Lord Mottistone) mounted on his horse Warrior. This helped Munnings to obtain the commission for a portrait of Lord Athlone in uniform and on horseback. Munnings commented that 'being a good likeness I sent it to the Royal Academy where it was hung in the first room'. This painting, in addition to the works of Canadian soldiers, led to many commissions which continued until the outbreak of the Second World War. These paintings demonstrated Munnings' ability to paint a rider's portrait as skilfully as he painted the horse and assured him of a flow of

ALFRED MUNNINGS

The Artist at Calcot Park Remount Depot, Reading

Pencil drawing on grey paper 235 x 200mm

SPINK AND SON, LONDON

LIONEL EDWARDS

Lady Munnings at a Meet of the Devon and Somerset Staghounds watching the Tufting, Cloutsham

Gouache 350 x 245mm

SPINK AND SON, LONDON

ALFRED MUNNINGS

The Barle near Brightworthy 1942

Oil on canvas

THE MUNNINGS TRUSTEES, DEDHAM, ESSEX

ALFRED MUNNINGS

Mill Hill, Oare 1939

Oil on canvas 760 x 915mm

ALFRED MUNNINGS

*Lady Munnings riding a Grey Hunter,
side saddle, with her dogs on Exmoor
1924*

Oil on canvas 1270 x 1015mm

commissions which brought him money and fame and took him into the society of the great houses, something beyond his wildest dreams as a young man in Cornwall.

Munnings was always at heart the Suffolk yeoman, a man of sturdy and independent character and total lack of affectation. He was also an egocentric wit and raconteur, an outspoken critic of avant-garde paintings and a friend of groom and statesman alike. He was a man who could not be ignored, the complete antithesis of Edwards who was quiet and gentle, but, like Munnings, lived for horses and his work.

In 1920 Munnings married Violet McBride, a renowned horsewoman who had won the Gold Cup at Olympia as well as many other prizes. A determined, astute and shrewd woman, with a firm belief in her husband's ability, she was a tremendous help in promoting his career. She attended to the business side of Munnings' work, effectively acting as his manager and agent, though she is on record as saying that 'he was never such a good artist after he married me'. The significance of this statement is that Munnings, rather than painting in the relaxed way to which he had become accustomed at Lamorna, was now very much a commercially-minded artist. He had both a London and country home, Castle House at Dedham in Essex, and this meant, in effect, painting for money. For twenty years he travelled extensively and worked extremely hard producing an enormous number of equestrian portraits of the highest quality, but his heart was always in Dedham and whenever possible he went back there, basically to obtain the freedom to paint landscapes which, with horses, were his abiding passion.

Looking through the pages of Munnings' autobiography it is obvious that his early love for Exmoor was never lost. He went there as often as he could together with his wife, for it continued to have a hold over him. He commented, 'This wild country is casting its net over me.' During the Second World War, Munnings' love for Exmoor induced him to stay for the duration (1940–45) at Hamilton House next to the church at Withypool. Here, free from the pressures of producing large numbers of equestrian portraits and racing set pieces, he was able to indulge his passion for landscape and animal painting, and over the four years produced an enormous quantity of paintings of Exmoor Horn sheep, Exmoor ponies and a large number of landscapes featuring the area immediately around Withypool.

He also indulged his taste for composing ballads, producing among others *Old Brandy* and *Cherry Bounce – A Ballad of Exmoor*, to complement *Larkbarrow Farm* composed in 1938 and *An Exmoor Lane*. Munnings always said that 'the West inspired him to write ballads'. It was his view that the best of Exmoor was to be found between Brendon, Larkbarrow and Oare, and he recorded this northern section of Exmoor in a series of startling and highly evocative landscapes. However, Munnings could not be entirely free from his past as a portrait painter. One afternoon a knock came on the front door of Hamilton House. Opening the door, Munnings found a young Guards' officer, Lord

Mildmay of Fleet. He had last seen him when painting him in the famous blue-and-white Mildmay racing colours on his horse 'Davey Jones', on which he was so unlucky not to win the 1937 Grand National. Lord Mildmay had not come to seek a portrait of himself in uniform but to find a hot bath! At that time Exmoor was being used as a training ground by the Guards' Armoured Brigade prior to their embarkation for Europe in the D-Day Landings. Lady Munnings was also a familiar figure on the moor and could often be seen exercising, from her horse, the Munningses' collection of dogs acquired from the Battersea Dogs Home. It was Lady Munnings' custom to attach them to her saddle by long strings and in this way she could exercise the animals while enjoying a quiet hack. In 1944 Munnings was elected President of the Royal Academy and, in the same year, was knighted by King George VI in the basement of Buckingham Palace.

At the end of the war Lionel Edwards staged something of a comeback with the new generation of buyers coming into the market. It had been noticeable during the late 1930s that much of his work was receiving negative approval or even criticism at London exhibitions. It was felt that his work was becoming both repetitive and, as far as the buying public was concerned, unattractive. After the war Edwards continued to paint extensively and to illustrate books including the children's classic, *Moorland Mousie*, as had been his practice in the past. His final painting on Exmoor was in 1963 when he painted the Devon and Somerset Staghounds coming out of the Danesbrook which lies in the south of the country and marks the boundary between Devon and Somerset. Three years later Edwards died at the age of 88.

For Sir Alfred Munnings the post-war years were a time of both controversy and reflection. He ceased to be President of the Royal Academy in 1949 and by that time had acquired a reputation as an implacable opponent of modern art, as it was then understood. In 1956 the Royal Academy held a retrospective exhibition of his paintings in the Diploma Gallery and shortly before that he finished the final volume of his autobiography. The three volumes cover reminiscences and observations on the English equestrian and artistic scene over some seventy years. He died in 1959 and engraved on the memorial tablet in the crypt of St Paul's Cathedral, are the words,

> *Oh friend how lovely are the things*
> *The English things, you helped us to perceive.*

Munnings, in a typical final gesture, left the pictures remaining in his possession to the nation for the encouragement of 'traditional art' and the remarkable collection can now be viewed at his home in Dedham.

Cecil Aldin has no memorial in St Paul's Cathedral. His memorial is more practical and more enduring. He was the first man to organise an all-children's pony show and gymkhana which was held on Cloutsham meadow and attended by 300 or so young riders. He and his hunting friends devised a number of competitions which became the standard part of children's gymkhanas. So successful was the event at Cloutsham that it was later moved to the fields below Dunster Castle and at the express wish of the then Prince of Wales, to Le Touquet. In addition, Cecil Aldin was also responsible for starting comic dog shows and terrier racing, inventing a mechanism for pulling the mock hare which, with variations, is still in use today.

Aldin, having pre-deceased his two fellow Exmoor sporting artists by some thirty years, was effectively forgotten by the 1960s and it was not until the early 1980s that a serious rediscovery and reappraisal of his work took place, primarily through the influence of Roy Heron's *Cecil Aldin, The Story of a Sporting Artist* and the Heale Gallery of Somerset.

During the 1930s a regular visitor to Exmoor was Denis Aldridge (1890–1985) with his wife, Kathleen, who shared the affection of their friends, Cecil Aldin and Lionel Edwards, for Exmoor and were often seen together at meets of the staghounds. Aldridge , a former secretary of the Quorn and of the South Atherstone Hunts, was a fine horseman and a talented artist who assisted Aldin, and later became an associate of Edwards, painting with him in Leicestershire and Hampshire. Some of his main subjects are deer, both on Exmoor and in Scotland. Arthur Wardle (1864–1949), the animal painter, also visited Exmoor. While having no formal art training, he took lessons from artists living near his childhood home in Chelsea and unlike most British sporting artists drew and painted every mammal from a mouse to an elephant, mostly at

MICHAEL LYNE

Found below Cloutsham

Oil on canvas 610 x 915mm

HEALE GALLERY, SOMERSET

MICHAEL LYNE

The Devon and Somerset Staghounds: Stag at Bay on the River Barle 1969

Oil on canvas 760 x 610mm

HEALE GALLERY, SOMERSET

London Zoo. His Exmoor work consisted of landscape and stag studies, no doubt for 'working up' in his studio at St John's Wood in London. Another artist to frequent the moor during the inter-war period was George Denholm Armour (1864–1949) who by that time was living at Sparkford near Yeovil in Somerset, and had built up a substantial reputation as a humorous sporting cartoonist for *Punch, The Sporting and Dramatic News* and similar publications.

Another visitor of that period, who was also primarily an illustrator, was Maurice Tulloch (1894–1974). Having spent the major portion of his life in the Indian army, he cultivated a compelling style as a pencil draughtsman, and following his retirement and return to England, studied for some time with the help of Lionel Edwards, beginning to use oils and actively seeking commissions for horse portraits. An extremely talented artist, though one whose work, by the short duration of his career, is extremely scarce and rarely seen. Another rare artist of that period is Thomas Ivester-Lloyd (1873–1942). A Liverpudlian by birth, Ivester-Lloyd was completely self-taught, except for a brief spell attending evening classes. During the First World War, in common with other artists, he served with the Remount Service and was subsequently commissioned into the Royal Artillery. In the post-war period he was engaged in painting 30 dioramas depicting battle scenes, in the British Empire Exhibition at Wembley in 1920. Subsequently he went on to illustrate, together with Baron Karl Reille, Sir John Buchanan Jardine's *Hounds of the World*, together with producing and illustrating his own book on hounds. He lived a precarious existence at Sherrington, Buckinghamshire, and acted as Master to the Sherrington Foot Beagles, his private pack.

The 1930s not only saw the established Exmoor artists working at the highest pitch, together with their friends and associates, but also new artists who would eventually take over from them. Michael Lyne (1912–89) was one such painter. He started visiting the moor around 1936 when his elder brother, John, had acquired a Lagonda sports car and they could travel to Exmoor from their Herefordshire home. Like his peers, Lyne absorbed the atmosphere of the moor and was greatly excited by it. One of his first pair of prints was of the Devon and Somerset Staghounds crossing a stream; its companion was the North Ledbury (his home pack) crossing a road.

In the late 1930s Lyne worked at full stretch. He held numerous exhibitions and received wide acclaim from the hunting and artistic press for the quality of his work and the freshness of his presentation. He was also, at that time, able to run his own private pack of beagles, the North Cotswold, subsequently to become the United Cotswold Beagles. He served in the Second World War and in 1946 took up the challenge of restarting his career. He did so with alacrity, feeling that he had six years' lost work to make up. This feeling stayed with him throughout his life and in part accounts for the high volume of his output; he followed in Sir Alfred Munnings' footsteps, establishing a strong United States market. Always given to experiment, his work is consequently of an uneven quality. On his day, he was absolutely superb, an artist who could be seldom bettered. The final decade of his life was spent in semi-retirement and he visited the moor regularly as he had always done. His painting of *A Stag at Bay* is, in the opinion of many, the best of its type.

Michael Lyne's contemporary, Peter Biegel (1913–87), did not begin to paint until he was twenty-five, when he became a student at Lucy Kemp-Welch's School. His studies were abruptly terminated by the war throughout which he served. A chance meeting with Lionel Edwards shortly after the war was to transform both his life and painting. Biegel was to attend a Medical Board in London and set off by train. Fearing that it would be impossible to obtain food, he had the forethought to take a large packet of sandwiches with him. During the journey up to London he noticed a tall, spare, elderly gentleman with a ring in the back of his bowler hat, looking rather upset after a fruitless search for a refreshment car. Biegel generously shared his sandwiches with the older man who turned out to be Lionel Edwards. During the course of the journey, Biegel's future was planned. Edwards recommended that Biegel should first take up figure drawing and to that end he attended Bournemouth School of Art. Afterwards he joined Edwards at Buckholt, the artist's Hampshire home. Biegel stayed with the Edwards family as a pupil in the tradition of the grand masters until 1948, when he left to marry and begin work on his own. The Biegels' honeymoon was spent on Exmoor and Peter Biegel took the opportunity to paint several pictures, one of which is a study of ponies.

According to tradition, one of the ways in which Biegel started his career was by taking his paintings around the Exmoor hunting pubs and showing them to hunting owners, in the hope of a sale or a commission. By the 1950s he was becoming well established, mainly through the efforts of Simon Wingfield Digby of Dorset, an established breeder of thoroughbreds. Like Michael Lyne, Biegel soon began visiting the United States, and for six years, from the late 1960s, he spent two months each year painting in North America. Through his friendship with Peter Payne-Gallwey, Peter Biegel became deeply interested in steeplechasers and steeplechasing, enabling him to produce some of his finest work, particularly paintings of the Grand National. Biegel, like Michael Lyne, retired early and the last years of his life were dogged by ill health.

The tradition of sporting art on Exmoor is still alive, thanks to the efforts of painters such as Donald Ayres and Robin Furness (Sir Stephen Furness) a Yorkshireman married to a Devonian who, whenever possible, visits Exmoor to paint. Many of his best works are to be found in Exmoor homes. Robin Furness draws his inspiration from the Northumbrian sporting artist and family friend, Tom Carr (1912–77) and it is pleasing to see one whose home and background is exclusively northern, painting the Exmoor scene with such freshness and vigour.

PETER BIEGEL

Exmoor Ponies (Mares and Foals) 1948

Oil on board 280 x 380mm

Painted during the artist's honeymoon

PRIVATE COLLECTION

ELLIS MARTIN

Cover designs for Ordnance Survey maps of Exmoor 1921

ORDNANCE SURVEY OFFICE

HENRY GEORGE WALKER

St Michael's, Minehead and Higher Town c.1925

Tinted etching 205 x 255mm

HEALE GALLERY, SOMERSET

While the hunting fraternity had a vested interest in the work of sporting artists, nevertheless their products had a wider market making Exmoor familiar to many who might otherwise have known nothing of its attraction other than the odd picture postcard from Minehead or Porlock. The market for the traditional topographical type of painting had partly diminished with the advent of the modern picture postcard and the type of topographical book which was produced in large quantities up until the 1920s and illustrated in colour by artists such as Ernest Haslehurst (1866–1949) and Alfred Quinton. An artist who continued this debased topographical tradition was Henry George Walker (fl.1921–31), a Birmingham etcher, who spent the whole of his professional life travelling the country in search of suitable material for popular views and subjects. Walker produced a number of etchings of Devon seaside towns, which by then had degenerated into family seaside holiday resorts and it was to this market that Walker addressed himself. A very competent artist, he produced pleasing scenes of no great originality, but acceptable as wall decoration by the visitors to the North Devon and Somerset coasts. The Devonian brothers, John and Louis Mortimer also sought to supply this market and produced innumerable watercolours of the coast, at prices which were highly attractive to visitors and available nationwide through the fine art department of Boots the Chemist, as were Cecil Aldin's later etchings! A slightly off-beat art form are the covers of the inter-war Ordnance Survey maps, two highly attractive views of Exmoor produced by Ellis Martin for the 1921 editions of O.S. maps of Exmoor.

Artists of heavier calibre included Lamorna Birch R.A., R.W.S. (1869–1955), the Newlyn artist, who regularly visited Exmoor and produced some highly attractive work of moorland villages and riverside scenes. Birch started life working in a Manchester cotton mill and sold his watercolour sketches in his spare time. He became a full-time artist at the age of twenty-seven, moving to Newlyn and then to study in Paris where he discovered the paintings of Monet and Pissaro. Returning to Newlyn, he took the name 'Lamorna' to avoid confusion with Lionel 'Newlyn' Birch, married (1902) and settled at Lamorna from where he travelled widely, reaching Australia and New Zealand. Possibly the most famous artist of all to visit the moor was Lucien Pissarro (1863–1944), the son of the French Impressionist painter, Camille Pissarro. Lucien spent most of his life in England and was in the habit of visiting friends on the Blackdowns, to the south-east of Exmoor, and occasionally visited the moor. He died in Axminster, Devon in 1944.

The only true, non-sporting, Exmoor artist of this final period was Alexander (Alec) Carruthers Gould R.B.A. (1870–1948). The son of Cecil Aldin's friend Sir Francis Carruthers Gould, Gould lived and worked in Porlock as an accomplished landscape and figure painter, exhibiting at all the major London exhibitions, including the Royal Academy and the New English Art Club, though he was never elected to the membership of either body, but was a member of the Chelsea Arts Club. He is

SAMUEL LAMORNA BIRCH

Old Bridge, June Day, Dulverton 1952

Oil on canvas 505 x 610mm

HENRY DUKE, FINE ART, DORCHESTER

ALEXANDER
CARRUTHERS GOULD

Dunkery

Watercolour 355 x 355mm

J. COLLINS AND SON, BIDEFORD

recorded as being educated privately, a fly fisher, fond of children and having worked during the First World War as a lumber man.

Since the Second World War, Exmoor has seen other artists. Only the perspective of history will show whether their work will prove to be of any value.

It is the quality of Exmoor's landscape, coast, valley and hill, that has led so many artists to visit and paint in the area. That this wild and beautiful landscape will endure is ensured since it is now in the expert custodianship of Exmoor National Park Authority. Whether the Authority, as an important landowner on the moor, will extend its activities to become a patron of the arts like the Aclands and Fortescues before it, remains to be seen.

ALEXANDER CARRUTHERS GOULD

Porlock from the Parks

Oil on panel 355 x 255mm

SOTHEBY'S, SUSSEX

APPENDIX

LIST OF PAINTERS WORKING ON AND AROUND EXMOOR

TOPOGRAPHICAL – ANTIQUARIAN – ROMANTIC

ABBOTT, John White *(1763–1851)*
ALLOM, Thomas *(1804–72)*
BAMPFYLDE, Coplestone Warre *(1720–91)*
BONNOR, T. *(fl.1791)*
BUCK, Samuel *(1696–1779)*
BUCK, Nathaniel *(fl. 1727–53)*
BUCKLER, John F.S.A. *(1770–1851)*
BUCKLER, John Chessell *(1793–1894)*
BUCKLER, E.H. *(fl.1855)*
BYRNE, Letitia *(1779–1849)*
CALLOW, William R.W.S. *(1812–1908)*
CHAMPION, George Bryant N.W.S. *(1796–1870)*
COLLINS, William R.A. *(1788–1847)*
COLLINSON, James *(1825–81)*
COOPER, Thomas Henry *(fl.1853)*
COX, David O.W.S. *(1783–1859)*
CRISTALL, Joshua P.O.W.S. *(1767–1847)*
DAVIS, William Henry *(c.1795–1885)*
DANIELL, William R.A. *(1769–1837)*
DE WINT, Peter O.W.S. *(1784–1849)*
DIBDIN, Charles *(fl.1745–1814)*
DUPONT, Gainsborough *(1754–97)*
FARINGTON, Joseph R.A. *(1747–1821)*
FEARY, John *(fl.1766–88)*
GAINSBOROUGH, Thomas R.A. *(1727–88)*
GARDINER, Tippetts H. *(fl.1774)*
GAUCI, W. *(fl.1820–40)*
HADLEY, J. *(fl.1730–58)*
HOLLAND, James O.W.S. *(1800–70)*
JACKSON, John *(1801–48)*
LANDSEER, Thomas A.R.A. *(1795–1880)*
LEWIS, Frederick Christian *(1779–1856)*
LEWIS, George Robert *(1782–1871)*
MARTIN, T. *(fl.1839–50)*
MULLER, William James *(1812–45)*
NICHOLSON, Francis O.W.S. *(1753–1844)*
PAYNE, William O.W.S. *(c.1760–1830)*
PHELPS, Richard *(c.1710–85)*
POCOCK, Nicholas O.W.S. *(1740–1821)*
PROUT, Samuel O.W.S. *(1783–1852)*
RACKETT, Rev. Thomas *(1757–1841)*

REED, L.E. *(fl.1830)*
ROWLANDSON, Thomas *(1756–1827)*
SAMUEL, George *(fl.1785–1823)*
SANDBY, Paul R.A. *(1725–1809)*
SHARLAND, R. *(fl.1830)*
SMITH, John 'Warwick' O.W.S. *(1749–1831)*
SPREAT, William *(fl.1820–50)*
SWETE, Rev. John *(c.1752–1821)*
SWEETING, Miss *(fl.1850)*
TOVEY, Samuel Griffiths *(fl. 1847–65)*
TOWNE, Francis *(1740–1816)*
TOWNSEND, G. *(fl.1854–60)*
TURLE, E. *(fl.1830)*
TURNER, Joseph Mallord William R.A. *(1775–1851)*
VIVIAN, Edward *(fl.1845)*
WESTALL, William A.R.A. *(1781–1850)*
WHEATLEY, William Walter *(1811–85)*
WILKINS, George *(fl.1830–55)*
WILLCOCK, George Barrell *(1811–52)*
WILLIAMS, Thomas Hewitt *(fl.1800–30)*
WILLIS, William *(fl.1845–57)*

NATURALISTIC – PICTURESQUE

ADAMS, Maurice Bingham *(1849–1933)*
BADGOOD, W. M. *(fl.1883)*
BRITTAN, Charles Edward Snr *(1837–1888)*
BRITTAN, Charles Edward Jnr *(b.1870)*
BUCKNALL, Ernest Pile *(1861–c.1919)*
CLARKE, Alfred Alexander *(1826–1913)*
COLLINS, Charles R.B.A. *(fl.1867–1903)*
COOPER, Alfred Heaton *(1863–1929)*
COX, David Jnr A.R.W.S. *(1809–85)*
CROWTHER, John *(fl.1876–98)*
DAWSON, Alfred *(fl.1860–93)*
DYER, William Henry *(fl.1890–1930)*
EDWARDS, P.E. *(did not exhibit)*
FRIER, Harry *(c.1849–1919)*
GASTINEAU, Henry G. O.W.S. *(1791–1876)*
GEORGE, Sir Ernest M.V.O., R.A., P.R.I.B.A. *(1839–1922)*
GIBBS, J.W. *(1854–1906)*
GOODWIN, Albert R.W.S. *(1845–1932)*

GREIG, Donald *(did not exhibit)*
HARRIS, George *(1847–c.1915)*
HARRIS, Henry *(1852–1926)*
HASLEHURST, Ernest William R.B.A., R.I.
　(1866–1949)
HEWETT, Frank *(fl.1903–1914)*
HODGSON, George *(1847–1921)*
HOLDER, Edward Henry *(fl.1864–1917)*
HOLMES, Sir Charles John V.P.R.W.S., F.S.A.
　(1868–1936)
HOOK, James Clarke R.A. *(1819–1907)*
JAMESON, J.A.H. *(fl.1884)*
JENKINS, George Henry *(1843–1914)*
KENNEDY, Joseph *(fl.1861–88)*
KING, Baragwaneth *(fl.1903–1914)*
LEE, Frederick Richard R.A. *(1794–1879)*
LEWIS, John Hardwick *(1842–1927)*
LEYMAN, Alfred *(1856–1933)*
LUTTRELL, Mary *(fl.1924–1928)*
MANDER, William Henry *(fl.1880–1922)*
MARKS, George *(fl.1876–1922)*
MONTBARD, Georges *(fl.1880–1903)*
MONTGOMERY, H. *(fl.1859)*
NORTH, John William A.R.A., R.W.S. *(1842–1924)*
PALMER, Arthur *(fl.1891–1935)*
PARR, Frederick *(fl.1920s–'30s)*
PARSONS, Arthur Wild *(1854–1931)*
PARSONS, Beatrice E. *(1870–1955)*
PEARSON, Cornelius *(1809–91)*
PENLEY, Aaron Edwin R.I., A.N.W.S. *(1807–70)*
PIKE, William Henry R.B.A. *(1846–1908)*
PINWELL, George John O.W.S. *(1842–75)*
PITT, William *(fl.1849–1890)*
PROUT, Samuel Gillespie *(1822–1911)*
PYNE, James Baker R.B.A. *(1800–70)*
QUINTON, Alfred Robert *(1853–1934)*
RIDGWAY, S.R. *(fl.1870)*
RIMINGTON, Alexander Wallace R.B.A. R.E.
　(1854–1918)
ROWE, George *(1797–1864)*
SCHOFIELD, John William R.I., R.B.A., R.B.C.
　(fl.1889–1944)
SCOUGALL, H.B. *(fl.1856)*
SHEPHERD, F.H.S. *(fl.1902–1938)*
SIDNEY, Thomas *(fl.1900s)*
SUKER, Arthur *(1857–86)*
SWEET, Walter Henry *(1889–1943)*
THRUPP, Frederick *(1812–95)*
TOWNSEND, Alfred O. *(fl.1888–1902)*
TYNDALE, Walter Frederick Roofe R.I., R.B.I.
　(1855–1943)
VACHER, Thomas Brittain *(1805–80)*
WALKER, Frederick A.R.A., O.W.S. *(1840–75)*
WATERHOUSE, Alfred R.A. *(1830–1905)*
WATSON, Alfred John *(fl.1904–22)*
WHITBY, W. *(fl.1886)*

WHITE, John R.I., R.O.I. *(1851–1933)*
WIDGERY, Frederick John *(1861–1942)*
WIDGERY, William *(1826–93)*
WINBUSH, Henry B. *(1861–1910)*

Twentieth Century

BADMIN, Stanley Roy R.W.S. *(b.1906)*
BEVAN, Robert Polhill *(1865–1925)*
BIRCH, Samuel John 'Lamorna' R.A., R.W.S.
　(1869–1955)
CHARLTON, Edward William R.E. *(fl.1890–1930)*
GOULD, Alexander (Alec) Carruthers R.B.A.
　(1870–1948)
HEARD, Hugh Percy *(1866–1940)*
LE BAS, Ann *(living artist)*
MORTIMER, Louis *(fl.1920–30)*
MORTIMER, John *(did not exhibit)*
MOSER, Robert Oswald R.I., R.O.I. *(1874–1953)*
PISSARRO, Lucien *(1863–1944)*
POWER, Harold Septimus *(fl.1908–35)*
SHAPLAND, John *(1865–1929)*
STANILAND, Lancelot Norman R.W.A. *(fl.1925–69)*
TUCKER, James Walker A.R.W.A. *(1898–1973)*
WALKER, Henry George *(fl.1921–31)*
WELLS, William *(fl.1893–1923)*
WHEELWRIGHT, Rowland R.B.A. *(1870–1955)*

Sporting 1880–1990

ALDIN, Cecil Charles Windsor R.B.A. *(1870–1935)*
ALDRIDGE, Denis *(1890–1985)*
ARMOUR, George Denholm O.B.E. *(1864–1949)*
AYRES, Donald (living artist)
BIEGEL, Peter *(1913–87)*
BLINKS, Thomas *(1853–1910)*
CHARLTON, John R.B.A., R.I., R.O.I. *(1849–1917)*
EDWARDS, Lionel Dalhousie Robertson R.I., R.C.A.
　(1878–1966)
FURNESS, Sir Stephen (Robin) Bart *(living artist)*
GUEST, Alison *(living artist)*
HALL, Frederick R.B.C., N.E.A.C. *(1860–1948)*
HALL, Herbert Byng *(fl.1849)*
IVESTER-LLOYD, Thomas *(1873–1942)*
KEMP-WELCH, Lucy R.I., R.O.I., R.B.A., R.C.A.
　(1869–1958)
LYNE, Michael *(1912–89)*
MUNNINGS, Sir Alfred James K.C.V.O., P.R.A.,
　R.W.S., R.P. *(1878–1959)*
SEALY, Allen Culpeper *(1850–1927)*
STRANG, William R.A. *(1859–1921)*
TULLOCH, Maurice *(1894–1974)*
WARDLE, Arthur *(1864–1949)*
WELLS, John Sanderson. R.I., R.B.A. *(fl.1872–1943)*

SELECT BIBLIOGRAPHY

Aldin, C., *The Romance of the Road*, 1928 (facsmilie 1986).
Time I Was Dead (autobiography), 1934.
Exmoor, The Riding Playground of England, 1935.
English Life – various articles.

Allen, N.V., *Churches and Chapels of Exmoor*, 1974.

Anderson, P.C., *Quicksilver – A Hundred Years of Coaching 1750–1850*, 1947.

Arts Council of Great Britain, *Welsh Landscape in British Art* (Exhibition Catalogue), 1947.

Ayrton, M., *British Drawings*, 1946.

Banfield, J. (Pub.), *Scenery in the North of Devon* (various artists), 1837.
A Guide to Ifracombe and the Neighbouring Towns, 1840.
Views of Lynton and Lynmouth (illus. W. Willis), 1850.
Banfield's Views of North Devon (illus. W. Willis), 1860.

Barley, M.W., *Guide to British Topographical Collections*, 1974.

Bates, A., *Directory of State Coach Services 1836*, 1969.

Berry, C., *The Racehorse in Twentieth-Century Art*, 1989.

Binding, H.M., *Discovering Dunster*, 1990.

Blackie and Son (Pub.), *Beautiful England* Series.

Blackmore, R.D., *Lorna Doone*, 1869.

Booth, S., *Sir Alfred Munnings* 1878–1959, 1986.

Bourne, H.L., *A Little History of Exmoor*, 1968.

Bradley, A.G., *Exmoor Memories*, 1926.

Bright, I.P. (Pub.), *Views of Ilfracombe*, 1860.

British Sporting Art Trust, *Twentieth Century Sporting Art* (Exhibition Catalogue), 1983.

Bunt, C.G., *Life and Work of W.J. Muller*, 1948.

Burlington Gallery, *Catalogues of Annual Cecil Aldin Exhibitions*.

Burton, S.H., *Exmoor*, 3rd edn. 1978.

Castle House, Dedham, *Catalogue of the 1994 Exhibition of Paintings by Sir Alfred Munnings K.C.V.O.*

Chadwyck-Healey, C.E.H., *The History of Part of West Somerset*, 1901.

Collins, J. and Son, *Autumn Exhibition (W. and F.J. Widgery) Catalogue*, 1993.

Collinson, Rev. J., *History and Antiquities of the County of Somerset*, 1791.

Coltman, *British Itinerary and Principal Crossroads of Great Britain*, 1811.

Coombs, D., *Sport and the Countryside*, 1978.

Cooper, T.H., *Guide Containing a Short Historical Sketch of Lynton and Places Adjacent in North Devon*, 1853.

Davies, E.W.L., *Memoir of the Rev. John Russell*, 1878.

Defoe, D., *Tour Through the Whole Island of Great Britain*, 1927 edn.

Devon and Somerset Staghounds, *Exhibition Catalogue of Sporting Pictures*, 1978.

Ditchfield, P.H., *Cottage and Village Life in Rural England*, 1912.

Dry, G., *Catalogue Raisonné of Robert Bevan Lithographs and Other Prints*, 1968.

Dunning, R.W., *A History of Somerset*, 1978.

Eardley-Wilmot, H., *Yesterday's Exmoor*, 1990.

Edwards, L., *A Sportsman's Bag*, 1937.
Reminiscences of a Sporting Artist, 1947.

Edwards, M., *Figures in a Landscape*, 1986.

Evered, P., *Staghunting with the D. and S., 1887–1901*, 1902.

Farr, G., *Somerset Harbours*, 1954.
West Country Passenger Steamers, 1967.

Finberg, A.J., *The English Watercolour Painters*, 1905.
Inventory of Drawings of the Turner Bequest, (Vol 2) 1909.

Ford, B. (ed.), *Cambridge Guide to the Arts in Britain: The Augustan Age*, 1991.
Romantics to Early Victorian, 1990.

Fortescue, J.W., *Records of Staghunting on Exmoor*, 1887.

Godfrey, R.T., *Printmaking in Britain*, 1978.

Graves, A., *Dictionary of Artists*, 1891 (facsimile 1969).

Gray,B., *The British Print*, 1937.

Greenwood, G.J., *Map of Exmoor*, 1822.

Hall, H.B., *Exmoor: or In the Footsteps of St Hubert in the West,* 1849.

Hamilton, A., *The Red Deer of Exmoor*, 1907.

Hann, A.C.O., *Somerset*, 1927.

Hardie, M., *English Coloured Books*, 1906.

Harper, C.G., *The Exeter Road*, 1899.
The Somerset Coast, 1909.

Hayes, J., *Gainsborough's Drawings*, (2 vols), 1970.

Hendy, E.W., *Wild Exmoor Through the Year*, 1930.

Heron, R., *Cecil Aldin: the Story of a Sporting Artist*, 1981.
The Sporting Art of Cecil Aldin, 1990.

Herrmann, L., *Turner's Prints*, 1990.
Turner, 1975.

Hestercombe House, Taunton, Sale Catalogue of Contents, 11 October, 1872.

Hinton, I.T., *Watering Places of Great Britain*, 1831.

Holloway, E., 'Sir Alfred Munnings at Withypool', *Exmoor Review*, Vol.35, 1994.

Holloway, M., *British Topographical Books with Steel Engraving*, 1977.

Hunt, P. (ed.), *Devon's Age of Elegance*, 1984.
Payne's Devon, 1986.

Jefferies, R., *Red Deer*, 1884.

Johnson, J., and A. Greutzner, *The Dictionary of British Artists*, 1880–1940, 1976.

Joyce, W.W. (ed.), *Moorside Tales and Talk*, 1935.

Lewis, F.C., *The Scenery of the River Exe*, 1827.

Lyne, M., *Horses, Hounds and Country*, 1938.

Madge, R., *Railways Round Exmoor*, 1988 edn.

Maton, W.G., *Observations Relative Chiefly to...the Western Counties of England*, Vol 2, 1797.

Maxwell, D., *Unknown Somerset*, 1912.

McDermot, E.T., *The Devon and Somerset Staghounds 1907–1936*, 1936.

Mee, A., *The King's England: Devon*, 1938.
The King's England: Somerset, 1940.

Messum, D., *Lucy Kemp-Welch,* 1976.

Miles, R., and Bonham-Carter, V., *The Exmoor Bibliography,* 1989.

Mitchell, S., *The Dictionary of Equestrian Artists*, 1985.

Munnings, A.J., *An Artist's Life*, 1950.
The Second Burst, 1951.
The Finish, 1952.

National Trust Guides, *Arlington Court*, 1992.
Dunster Castle, 1993.
Killerton, 1978.
Knightshayes Court, 1992.

Newton, E., *British Painting*, 1945.

North Devon Museum, *Exhibition Catalogue of Devon Paintings*, 1994.

Northcote, Lady R., *Devon: Its Moorlands, Streams and Coasts*, 1908.

Page, J.W., *An Exploration of Exmoor and the Hill Country of West Somerset*, 1890.
The Rivers of Devon, 1893.

Paterson, D., *Direct and Principal Crosss Roads in Great Britain*, 1771 (18th edn,1829).

Pendred, G.L., *An Inventory of British Sporting Art*, 1987.

Pevsner, N., *Buildings of England: Devon*, 1989 edn.
Buildings of England: South and West Somerset, 1958.

Presland, J., *Lynton and Lynmouth*, 1918.
Prideaux, S.T., *Aquatint Engraving*, 1909.

Rawle, E.J., *Annals of the Ancient Royal Forest of Exmoor*, 1893.

Rawlinson, W., *Turner's Liber Studiorum*, 1906. *The Engraved Work of J.M.W. Turner*, 1908.

Redgrave, R., *Dictionary of Artists of the English School*, 1878.

Reed, L.E., *Views on the River Exe*, c.1830.

Rowe, G., *The Beauties of the North of Devon*, c.1828. *Views of North Devon*, c.1835. *Scenery in the North of Devon*, c.1835. *Views in North Devon*, c.1840.

Russell, R., *Guide to British Topographical Prints*, 1979.

Rutter, J., *Delineations of North West Somerset*, 1829.

Savage, J., *History of the Hundred of Carhampton*, 1830.

Shanes, E., *Turner's England*, 1990. *Turner's Picturesque Views in England and Wales 1825–1838*, 1979.

Simmons, J. ed., *Journeys in England*, 1951.

Smiles, S., and Pidgley, M., *The Perfection of England*, 1995.

Snell, F.J., *A Book of Exmoor*, 1903.

Somers Cocks, J.V., *Devonshire Topographical Prints 1660–1870*, 1977.

Speed, J., *The Counties of England*, rep.1993.

Spink and Son Ltd., *Twentieth Century British Sporting Pictures: Catalogues of the 1985 and 1987 Exhibitions.*

Spreat, W., *Picturesque Sketches of the Churches of Devon*, 1842. *Views of the Scenery in North Devon*, 1850.

Stephens, W., *The Guiness Guide to Field Sports*, 1978.

Stoddard, S., *Mr Braikenridge's Brislington*, 1981.

Sweeting, Miss, *Sketches of Scenery in West Somerset*, 1850.

Tate Gallery, *Turner: The Third Decade*, (Exhibition Catalogue). *Turner: Painting and Poetry*, (Exhibition Catalogue). *Paintings by Robert Bevan 1865–1925*, (Exhibition Catalogue), 1956.

Travis, J.F., *The Rise of the Devon Seaside Resorts, 1750–1900*, 1993.

Tristram, W.O., *Coaching Days and Coaching Ways*, 1924.

Tugwell, Rev. G., *The North Devon Handbook*, (illus. Willis), 1855. *The North Devon Scenery Book*, (illus. Scougall), 1856.

Vowles, A., *Lorna Doone Country*, 1930.

Vivian, E., *Sketches in North Devon*, 1845.

Walker, S., *British Sporting Art in the Twentieth Century*, 1989.

Warren, C.H., *West Country*, 1938.

Ward Lock and Co., *Guide to Lynton, Lynmouth and Minehead*, 1890.

Waterhouse, E., *British Eighteenth-Century Painters*, 1981.

Whybrow, C., *Antiquary's Exmoor*, 1970.

Wilenski, R.H., *An Outline of English Painting*, 1933.

Williams, T.H., *A Tour to the North of Devon, 1802. A Guide to the Picturesque Scenery and Antiquities of Devonshire*, 1827–8.

Wilson, R.B., *Go Great Western*, 1970.

Wood, C., *Paradise Lost*, 1988. *The Dictionary of Victorian Painters*, 1978.

Wood, J., *Hidden Talents*, 1994.

Woodspring Museum, *The Smyth-Pigott Family Portraits.*

Yeates, J., *Michael Lyne: Sporting Artist*, 1992.

INDEX